Optimism: The How and Why

By Victor Perton

Printed 2019

ISBN: 9781686098376
Imprint: The Centre for Optimism

Preface

At its simplest, optimism is an expectation that good things will happen and that things will work out in the end.

There's strong evidence that optimism will improve your health. There is a strong link between optimism and longevity. Infectious optimism is the key trait of the globally successful leader.

In her introduction to my book, "The Case for Optimism: The Optimists' Voices", Helen Clark, former New Zealand Prime Minister and Administrator of the United Nations Development Programme said:

"Good things happen when good people get together in common cause. More than 200 people have shared their wisdom and insights in this book 'The Case for Optimism.' Their views are fresh and sparkle off the pages which follow. Most will inspire, some will amuse and others look to improve the current state of global leadership. Certainly, this is excellent thought-provoking material to share in conversations and speeches for adults and children alike."

In my workshops on infectious optimistic leadership, the strongest feedback was "enough about why to be optimistic, I want to know how to become more optimistic." Others wanted to know how to build more optimism in their teams, businesses and families.

For those looking to become more optimistic, this book will help you on your path to being more optimistic.

For the optimists, this book will bring a smile to your face, help you to be more infectiously optimistic and support the wellbeing of those around you.

Victor Perton
October 2019

Table of Contents

Introduction: The Case for Optimism

In 2018, following a strong positive reaction to a presentation by me on the Case for Optimism, I wrote and published the book "The Case for Optimism: The Optimists' Voices."

Following the publication of that book, I was struck by people's desire to learn more about how to be optimistic and the yearning for stories of optimism and hope.

I made asking the question "what makes you optimistic?" into a habit - meeting people formally and informally in interviews, on the street and on social media. For most people, it's the first time they have been asked about their optimism.

I presented the case for optimism in keynote speeches, workshops, roundtables and retreats in corporate environments, universities, schools, community groups and in prison.

This book answers the needs expressed in the feedback from those sessions and meetings.

Presented with the evidence of the positive impact of optimism on mental and physical health and in the world of work, people quickly get the case for optimism.

People ask, "How do I become more optimistic?"

They want to know how to do it. Parents want to generate greater optimism in their children. Employers want to create more confidence in their workforce. Employees want their bosses to be more optimistic. Children want their teachers to be infectiously optimistic.

In these times of pessimism and cynicism, optimism is sometimes is met with cynicism and doubt.

People have told me:

"I am an optimist but criticised for being unrealistic: What do I do?"

"I have a very negative person in my weekly meetings bringing down the morale of the team; what do I do?"

There are answers to these questions in this book.

My questions for you:

When did you last ask your spouse, partner, parents or children, "What makes you optimistic?"

Have you ever used the phrase "I am optimistic about..." in a business or strategy meeting?

Why don't you try it before you read on? Ask someone else, "What makes you optimistic?"

Most people are surprised at how asking the question lifts the person asked and the questioner.

Give it a go!

The Benefits of Greater Optimism

If optimistic, you will feel healthier. An optimistic spirit can bring significant benefits, including happiness, joy, active longevity, better health including lower risks of cardiovascular disease, better sleep, greater resilience, stronger relationships and increased self-mastery.

A recent OECD Study on Social and Emotional Skills in schools found, "Emotional stability skills are found to be the most predictive of mental health. Optimism has the highest relation to life satisfaction scores"

Optimism may help you live longer.

Research by several leading American universities and centers, have established a very strong link between optimism and longevity. As Dr Carol Graham of the Brookings Institution said, "The link between optimism and longevity is strong."

Why? It is believed that optimistic people are better able to balance their emotions more effectively and that they more easily bounce back from some of the many stresses that life offers.

Optimism is strongly linked to a lower risk of cardiovascular events. A 2018 study by the American College of Cardiology attributes this in part to the fact that "Optimists persevere by using problem-solving and planning strategies to manage stressors."

A 2019 University of Illinois study shows people who are the most optimistic tend to be better sleepers. Again, as the lead researcher Professor Rosalba Hernandez said, "Optimists are more likely to engage in active problem-focused coping and to interpret stressful events in more positive ways, reducing worry and ruminative thoughts when they're falling asleep and throughout their sleep cycle...Dispositional optimism—the belief that positive things will occur in the future—has emerged as a psychological asset of particular salience for disease-free survival and superior health."

The Resilience Project's Founder, Hugh van Cuylenburg, says "An optimist is less likely to die from infection, cancer, heart disease, stroke and respiratory disease. Optimists are also likely to enjoy better levels of mental health. Science shows optimists are significantly more successful than pessimists in aversive events and when unforeseen circumstances get in the way of achieving important life goals."

Professor Dianne Vella-Brodrick puts it well, "When it comes to health, positive psychology goes beyond the idea that wellness is simply the absence of illness and instead looks at the body as a complete system. Along with being disease-free – indeed, research shows that being optimistic is linked to improved heart health, – positive health is defined by less frequent and briefer ailments, greater recuperative ability and rapid wound healing. What's more, people who experience positive emotions are more likely to live longer than people who are less happy (but not depressed)."

Optimism helps you function better as a leader. In my work with the Australian Leadership Project, it's clear that optimistic leaders have a clear advantage in the Australian culture and beyond.

I recently has the opportunity to interview the global leader of positive psychology Professor Martin Seligman on what makes him optimistic. On this point, Martin says, "The defining characteristic of pessimists is that they tend to believe bad events will last a long time, will undermine everything they do, and are their own fault. The optimists, who are confronted with the same hard knocks of this world, think about misfortune in the opposite way. They tend to believe defeat is just a temporary setback, that its causes are confined to this one case. The optimists believe defeat is not their fault: Circumstances, bad luck, or other people brought it about. Such people are unfazed by defeat. Confronted by a bad situation, they perceive it as a challenge and try harder."

In another study, social psychologists Lise Solberg Nes and Suzanne Segerstrom found that optimists were more likely to take charge and find ways to solve their problems than pessimists were. They chose coping strategies such as seeking out emotional support, drawing on spiritual resources, or just becoming more accepting of their situation. They also chose not to run away from their problems.

Optimism is the underpinning for innovation, entrepreneurship and creativity. These callings require resilience, experimentation and the understanding that failed experiments are on the pathway to success.

The recently retired head of the Australian Prime Minister's Department Dr Martin Parkinson put this well when he told me, "Optimism drives curiousity which in turn fosters innovation and invention. So whatever the challenges we face, it's better to tackle them with an optimistic bent, confident that nothing is insurmountable given enough will and effort."

My Optimism?

I have been a lifelong optimist. Like most optimists, I have my share of grief and failure, but I always think that things will work out alright in the end.

I was born in Australia and am fortunate that the traumas suffered by my ancestors and family on the way to Australia strengthened them and their realistic optimism. My grandparents and parents faced Soviet terror with courage, and the family survived through optimism and persistence. My paternal grandfather was tortured to death. My paternal grandmother was sent to the Gulag. My maternal grandparents and parents were refugees facing death on several occasions.

My paternal grandmother was a great example to me. After surviving the Gulag, Bronislava was determined to outlive communism and participated in the civil disobedience which led to the 1991 collapse of the Soviet Union.

Most importantly, I have the lifelong influence of my mother, Lilia, who showed great courage and resilience when my father passed away after a short illness when I was eight. She says that yoga practice and meditation helped her to manage life with optimism and strength.

Thinking about how I enhance my optimism, I am very grateful for the circumstances in which I live.

My children and I engage in daily gratitude practices. And, of course, it's always nice to be on the receiving end of other people's gratitude.

I meditate in several styles from simple breathing exercises to guided meditation to using mantras. I do yoga but could always do with more. I enjoy the beauty of nature and try to rise before dawn to enjoy the colours of the dawn, which, if exceptional, I take photos and share with family and friends and on social media.

As advised in my writings and speeches, I have turned down the news and use carefully selected search agents to find the good news that's interesting to me. I am fortunate to have family and friends share materials with me. Of course, I don't want to be a hermit, so I keep in touch with mainstream news services despite the overwhelming pessimism they propagate.

I enjoy humour and cartoons and most days listen to and search out some jokes and tell some jokes. My preference is for the Australian tradition of self-effacing humour.

And, of course, I have the advantage that almost every day, I ask people what makes them optimistic and share those answers with the world. That's uplifting and joyful.

Now onwards.

The book is divided into two parts. Part 1 is the "How To." Part 2 The Optimists Voices consists of the inspiring and informative quotes from hundreds of people who have answered my question "What makes you optimistic?

Read Part 1 at any pace. My suggestion is that Part 2 is a page a day book to lift you at home, work or school.

Part 1: How to become More Optimistic

Optimism Can be Learned

The good news? Optimism can be learned, developed and increased at any age!

Exercises and practices which increase and maintain optimism include expressing gratitude, using more positive language and focusing on sharing happiness. Practising meditation, yoga, exercise and spending time in beautiful places also enhance a feeling of optimism.

The science of neuroplasticity shows that our brains constantly make new connections and we strengthen positive neural networks by looking for the positives in life and by deliberately cultivating optimistic thoughts and words.

What makes you optimistic?

Yes, it's the opening question. Surrounding yourself with optimistic people, listening to optimistic people, being part of an optimistic team all increase your optimism but it comes down to YOU!

What makes you optimistic?

Put this book aside and take a paper, device or keyboard and write down "What makes me optimistic? I'm optimistic because xxxxxxx"

Fill in the xxxxx

If you have filled in the xxxx, keep a copy folded in this book. If you are pleased with this first cut, turn it into a poster, post-it note or write a message in lipstick or texta on your mirror.

If you haven't filled in the xxxx, have a think. Do the advances in your workplace or profession give you a sense that things are getting better? Science and healthcare are getting every better. Communications technology is advancing at incredible rates.

Take a break, open up Part 2 of this book and have a read of what some other people say makes them optimistic.

Ask Others "What makes you optimistic?"

People ask what makes me optimistic. There's a long list of facts and human advances that drive and reinforce my optimism. But the central thing that starts my day is an email and social media in-tray which includes people answering my question to them "what makes you optimistic?" I share those answers in various formats including social media, blogging and in books like this one.

Why don't you try it? Ask a colleague, friend or family member "what makes you optimistic?"

Generally, they will be cheered by answering and considering their own case for optimism. So will you!

Occasionally you have to persist. A father who followed my advice asked his wife and children what makes them optimistic. He sent me the answers from his wife and daughter but his 16-year-old son had told him to "Get XXXXXX". I suggested he leave it a month or two.

Some people will say, nothing makes me optimistic! Maybe that's true, they're a pessimist. But if you persist without being annoying, they will eventually find some reason. Maybe share some of the reasons from Part 2 of this book.

Early one morning I met an engineer in Delhi, India, who looked a little sad. I asked him the question to which he responded "nothing." We talked a little longer including some reasons for optimism. The next morning at breakfast, I suddenly heard a large voice calling "Vince, Vince." The engineer told me I had changed his whole day and his outlook for the fortnight in India.

He couldn't remember my name but he remembered how I had made him feel.

So take a break from the book. Go and ask someone "What makes you optimistic?" Face to face is best but a phone call or electronic message will work out! If the answer inspires, turn it into a poster and send it back to them. Think about posting it on social media (with their consent).

Optimism is a Strength not a Weakness

One of the questions I get during the Q&A after keynote speeches is from people feeling they are ridiculed or diminished in their optimism and what should they do about it.

The loudest voices at their board table, executive meeting or team meeting are those complaining, being pessimistic and bemoaning the lack of leadership around them.

Some of these people conform to a pessimistic conversation model, suppressing their optimism for fear of becoming labelled Pollyanna or unrealistic.

True optimists and realistic optimists do not ignore challenges, the bad stuff or pretend that negative feelings and experiences do not exist.

The true optimist acknowledges those challenges and then says, "I can work through those!"

****

Surround yourself with Optimists

Optimism, like pessimism, is infectious. So make a point to maximise your time spent with optimistic people.

Negative and pessimistic people sap your energy. There will be times when you have to spend time with them - they may be family, old friends and work-colleagues. However, try to spend the rest of your time with positive and optimistic people.

Generally, optimists attract other optimists, and those other optimists will boost your own optimism, joy and happiness. It can become a virtuous circle, but you first need to seek it out or set it up.

Choose your company wisely and limit the time you spend with people who do not fill your cup of optimism and self-confidence. Lead the conversation with positive questions. Prepare for gatherings by bringing to mind positive stories you have heard or read recently.

Meghan, Duchess of Sussex says "it's so important to surround yourself with people who are grounded and really optimistic."

Paul Wheelton AM KSG told me, "My success in business has come about by only associating with positive people. Avoid the glass half empty people - they drain your energy and turn your imagination off. Make a decision at the start of every day to be the glass half full person and before too long you are hard wired for success."

Gordon Tredgold says, "Surround yourself with positive people and see their optimism give you the strength to try new things"

Good Questions and Answers

Use positive language to foster the positive change you think we need. Be optimistic.

You can develop a more optimistic attitude and manner by practising positive speech and actions every day and all day.

Ask Better Questions

How to raise the optimism around you? One way? Ask better questions.

In Australia, as in France and many other countries, on meeting or passing someone, people routinely ask a question, "How are you?"

The answer, more often than not, is the double negative "not too bad."

Usually, it's ignored. The conversation moves on, or the people walk past each other without exchanging another question.

Think about what you ask people when you greet them.

Think about the answer you use.

Experiment: Next time you are in a position to interact with someone with a greeting, why don't you try replacing "How are you" with "What's the best thing happening for you?" or whatever similar question feels natural. If that works well, why not try it for a week?

Experiment: If someone asks you, "How are you?", pause… and respond with something like "Thank you for asking, life's good, and I am working on a very interesting…." Try this for one week.

I am willing to bet that an answer like that will cause them to pause and ask you an excellent question as a follow-up creating better engagement and, perhaps, making a new ally or friend.

Recently I shared this advice with a group of students at the University of Melbourne. One of the students kindly messaged me with "With mum, I asked her what the best thing was to happen to her today, and she absolutely loved it. Has been a very refreshing technique to use indeed. She has taken it back to (the) Law School, where she works and is finding it quite powerful to stimulate more meaningful conversations with her colleagues."

Try these changes in language for a week, and I would be delighted if you let me know how it goes.

****

Positive Self-Talk

A big part of learning to be more optimistic is positive self-talk. Empower yourself.

All of us feel anxious and worried at some time. Some of us feel more anxious and more sadness than others. It's in times of anxiety and sadness that it's more important than ever to reaffirm your desire to be more optimistic.

Where pessimists see problems, optimists may see opportunities. If you change the way you look at issues and challenges, your problems may diminish in importance and can transform into opportunities to learn and discover your inner-strengths.

Mistakes and second-best-results are opportunities for you to learn, not failures for you to endure. Don't take setbacks personally - they happen to everyone.

As the author R.H. Lewis said to me, "Our voice is the only voice in our head. What we say makes us optimistic or pessimistic. The choice is ours."

If you find yourself preoccupied with a problem, feeling negative, or experiencing self-doubt, change your focus by asking:

What part of the problem is in my control? Acknowledge what you can and cannot control. The things that are out of your control are out of your control. Focus on what you can change.

What's one thing I can do that might make the situation better or solve the problem?

What positive and productive ideas do I have about overcoming or managing the situation?

What resources do I have to overcome the threat or situation?

What are the opportunities presented to me by the situation?

Does the situation provide an opportunity for me to learn more about my strengths and positive qualities?

Can I find humour in the situation? Can I reduce the tension with a joke?

In a world of 7 billion people, does anyone really care about this mistake or setback?

What would God say if he was looking over my shoulder?

If you want to develop as an infectiously optimistic leader, use variations of these questions to empower your team and colleagues to think differently. Always remember, the leader looks like the person in your mirror.

****

Read Some Optimism Every Day

As I said earlier, people ask me what makes me optimistic. There are many things and my optimism grows daily as I share the optimism of friends, colleagues and strangers who answer my question, "What makes you optimistic?"

Part 2 of this book contains hundreds of affirmations and there are many people who read a page a day from my earlier books.

I get a lot of positive correspondence and mentions for sharing my thoughts and the thoughts of others on the benefits of optimism. Delivering one of my workshops in prison, a murderer told me why he had come to my workshop. His cellmate had come to a previous workshop and had a copy of my book - the cellmate now keeps a gratitude journal, reads one page of my book daily and lifts the spirits of his fellow prisoners. This prisoner wanted a deeper dose of that optimism directly from me. You can imagine how good that made me feel - changing one life through my commitment to spreading optimism.

So my advice is that you should read positive affirmations.

Obviously, I commend my collection but there are many other themed books and social media sites with beautiful writing stirring the optimistic and joyful parts of your brain and spirit.

Write Positive Affirmations

Reading the thoughts of others is positive - imagine the greater strength of focusing on your own wisdom and insights and writing them down.

There's evidence that it is a way of lifting yourself and those around you.

Share them with others face-to-face and on social media when you feel the quality merits it.

Writing down short statements can help remind you of your strengths.

While I don't like yellow post-its, many people do and you can leave those affirmations in places to help you, family and friends.

An experiment: What about a post-it or a message on your mirror reminding you that "The Leader looks like the person in my mirror" or more simply "I am an optimist."

Another experiment: Visualise your best possible self and imagine a future in which all you go*als* have been achieved. Write it in your journal.

Most experts on writing positive affirmations recommend that you choose one negative thought you have about yourself and write down the positive opposite that counteracts that belief. It's worth a try too.

Practise Gratitude

Gratitude is one of the underpinnings of optimism. While striving to reach our goals, it's important to feel grateful for what we have today.

The science on this is clear. Respected university studies have shown that habits of being consciously thankful make people more optimistic for an extended time and more optimistic about their lives in general.

Writing a few sentences each week or day is enough.

The American army uses a "Hunt for the good stuff" training exercise in which soldiers are encouraged to search for and focus on what they can be grateful for.

Action: Take a piece of paper or start a new document on your computer and list the things you are grateful for. Keep it somewhere easily found and go back to that list in a week and see what you can add to it.

Daily Gratitude Reflections

Late in the day, spend a few minutes reviewing everything that went right for you that day–even the small things. What did you enjoy? What felt validating? This type of reflection can help you program positive thoughts and images into your minds for the night. It may help you sleep better and awake more ready to face the day.

Ideally, keep a journal - best in hard-copy - buy a beautiful or elegant notebook for this purpose. Some people prefer to keep this as a file on their computer or smart-phone, that's fine too - whatever works best for you.

Professor Martin Seligman's authentic formula for this is:

"Every night for the next week, set aside ten minutes before you go to sleep. Write down three things that went well today and why they went well. You may use a journal or your computer to write about the events, but it is important that you have a physical record of what you wrote. The three things need not be earthshaking in importance ("My husband picked up my favorite ice cream for dessert on the way home from work today"), but they can be important ("My sister just gave birth to a healthy baby boy").

"Next to each positive event, answer the question "Why did this happen?" For example, if you wrote that your husband picked up ice cream, write "because my husband is really thoughtful sometimes" or "because I remembered to call him from work and remind him to stop by the grocery store." Or if you wrote, "My sister just gave birth to a healthy baby boy," you might pick as the cause ... "She did everything right during her pregnancy." Writing about why the positive events in your life happened may seem awkward at first, but please stick with it for one week. It will get easier."

Personally, I have adapted Seligman's three blessings to use on a daily basis and my family and I share three good things that went well over dinner.

Meditation

Meditation enhances your optimism. Meditations on optimism and related topics can strengthen your optimism even more.

The scientific evidence is that meditation practice results in long-lasting positive psychological effects. The research using brain scanning and other measures show meditation alters the structure of the brain, fostering a brighter more optimistic outlook and increased empathy. Over time, meditation thickens the bilateral, prefrontal right-insular region of the brain, the area responsible for optimism and a sense of well-being, spaciousness, and possibility. This area is also associated with creativity and an increased sense of curiosity, as well as the ability to be reflective and observe how your mind works. Regular sessions of meditation have a calming effect on the amygdala, the brain's emotion processor and reduce impulsive reactions to stressful or negative thoughts.

In other words, meditation practice gives you the much-needed rest to start afresh. Meditation will make you feel recharged and raring to go. You will be full of optimism and positivity. A Canadian study showed "Giving children mindfulness attention training in combination with opportunities to practice optimism, gratitude, perspective-taking, and kindness to others can not only improve cognitive skills but also lead to significant increases in social and emotional competence and well-being in the real-world setting of regular elementary classrooms."

There are many different ways to meditate, such as using a mantra (a word or phrase repeated), looking at an object, or focusing on the breath. It can be done sitting still or moving around while maintaining self-awareness.

Loving Kindness Meditation

Ancient meditation practices like the "Loving Kindness" meditation and related compassion meditations are particularly beneficial. Compassion meditation strengthens the connection between the prefrontal cortex and the brain's circuits for optimism, joy and happiness. The benefits are apparent right from the beginning of meditation practice and they increase with time spent.

By opening your heart and mind, meditation provides lasting feelings of peace and serenity while creating tremendously positive changes in your life. **Staying positive**, and its array of life-transforming benefits, can be easily learned and integrated into your life starting right now!

My loving kindness meditation is available on iTunes and other platforms.

Meditation on Optimism

You can meditate with a focus on optimism.

My simple meditation on optimism is available on iTunes and other platforms including YouTube.

Mindfulness

What is mindfulness? It's an ever-present meditation. As the Indian meditation teacher Sister Shivani told me her morning meditation prepares her for a mindful day.

While optimism is a belief that things will work out, one of the ways to increase and maintain your optimism is to stay more focused on the present.

Mindfulness reduces anxiety. Don't ruminate about the past or worry about what happens in an hour. Be intentional. Live in and concentrate on the moment.

Work on being present in each conversation, meeting and each interaction with others. Be your best in every moment, knowing that focus in the now will result in an even more positive future.

Jeanette Jifkins shared this advice with me. "Learn to appreciate the small, everyday occurrences in life and you will find optimism comes easily. Notice the way a soft breeze feels against your cheek, take a moment to listen to bird song, look up at the blue of the sky, smile for no reason. So much of our concern comes from modern lifestyles, get back to basics and you can't help but be surprised at the wonder in life."

It's well put and a good start.

Yoga and Exercise

This is an interesting factor - there's lots of jolly fat people who lift the feeling in the room and make other people feel optimistic.

However, in general, optimism is easier when you feel good. Healthy body, healthy mind is rooted in old wisdom and modern science.

The healthier you are, the more optimistic you'll be, and the more optimistic you are, the healthier you'll be.

Factors that interfere with one's ability to maintain a good mood and positive energy include lack of sleep, depleted energy from poor eating and lifestyle habits, and too little exercise.

My mother Lilia Perton, who has practiced yoga for over 50 years, advises "Daily practice of yoga and meditation are ways of achieving an optimistic mindset and presence. We can light up the room and light up the lives of people around us with a positive manner, mode of speech and a smile. I am so fortunate to have been a Yoga teacher for 50 years and inspire others to spread light, love, peace and optimism into the world."

Sarvesh Shashi told me, "Yoga teaches you how to be in the present and makes you understand how we can't undo the past and the future is yet to happen. So, live in the now. And in the now, there is only Optimism. Yoga enhances your ability to understand and comprehend that everything happens for a reason."

There are many types of yoga nowadays. If you haven't practised before I would commend an integral yoga teacher or a hatha yoga teacher.

Walk like an Optimist

As we have said, the mind and the body have an intrinsic connection. Each has a profound impact on the other.

If you are struggling to move your mind into a more positive perspective, try moving your body there first.

Stand up straight, shoulders back, chin held high, stretching your arms out as wide as they can go. Feel powerful. Feel positive.

Go for a walk. Make eye contact with passing people. Greet them with a cheery hello.

Carrying yourself with "positive posture" will encourage your mind to feel more positive as well.

Dance Like an Optimist

If walking like an optimist feels good, imagine dancing like an optimist. I keep a playlist of happy music and optimistic music. It lifts me and it could lift you too.

Some mornings, I exercise and dance to Pharrell's 'Be Happy' and August Green's 'Optimistic.'

Feel free to use my Optimism Playlist on iTunes. Make your own happy music playlist.

Happiness and Humour

Is happiness the underpinning of optimism or is optimism an underpinning of happiness? It doesn't matter - we know happier people tend to be more optimistic.

Smile

Just smile. Smile at other people. Smile at yourself in the mirror. If necessary, fake it till you make it.

Never underestimate the power of a smile.

We know that smiling stimulates brain patterns which reinforce feelings of happiness and optimism.

Laughter and Humour

Life may have many difficulties, but there's usually a funny side to every situation.

My cousin Karina Wegner is a psychologist in Australia's sub-tropical Hervey Bay. Karina's well-researched expert opinion is that "you should have as much fun as possible and laugh as much as you can. When you couple these together, you should be able to keep 'depression' (what they now call the disease of the 21st century) away. When you enjoy yourself and laugh, you will increase the serotonin levels in your body, thereby decreasing the risk of depression. When my clients leave my office in

Queensland's Hervey Bay, my practice manager makes sure the client is laughing or at least smiling before they leave. I have a waiting list of near three months and my clients travel long distances to see the "Optimistic Psychologist."

University studies have shown laughter can improve your immune system. increase disease fighting antibodies and lower inflammation in the body. Laughter increases heart rate and blood flow, and has similar health benefits to exercising. Endorphins are released during laughter, which helps to relieve pain, reduce cravings and stress, and slow the ageing process.

Humour can alleviate feelings of stress and depression.

It's not always easy but when family and colleagues test your patience, put a smile on your face - even forced ones help. Try to find the humor in the situation and make a light-hearted comment. Not always easy, but give it a go!

In Part 2 of this book, there's a chapter on the humour of optimism which may help lighten your mood and put people at ease as you become more of an infectious optimist.

Otherwise, go out and buy a book of jokes or dust off those joke books gathering dust on your bookshelves.

Turn Down The "News"

For decades while in politics, I was fixed into a daily cycle of listening to the news and responding by way of press release and commentary. While I was able to maintain my optimistic nature in the face of the pessimism of the daily news, it is undoubtedly a cause of pessimism, cynicism and even depression for many people.

As the President of Envision Kindness Dr David Fryburg said "Every day, people are exposed to negative images, stories, and experiences, We know that this exposure is stressful to the viewer—it causes anger, anxiety, depression, and can affect behavior, disconnecting people from one another.

Over the last 50 years, the news has become increasingly negative. Most newsrooms operate under three principle editorial rules, "if it bleeds it leads," "Bad News is Good News" and emphasise stories which sow "dissension, discord and disharmony." On television news, optimistic news is generally restricted to the fluffy animal story after the weather or during sports news.

The author Pico Iyer wrote, "So why am I an optimist? Partly because I've been working in the mainstream media for 35 years now, and I know not to trust it. It's always a single act of brutality that captures headlines, while a hundred acts of everyday kindness are ignored, and more and more, in the global neighborhood, our "news" is just the equivalent of small-town gossip. We're living in the age of Pope Francis and the Dalai Lama and more charitable efforts than ever before, but it'll always be the Las Vegas gunman or the ISIS operative with a knife who knows how to dominate our attention. My optimism comes from a deeper source, though, than simply knowing that what we hear and read isn't a fair register of what is really happening. As a traveller, I witness everyday people whose lives are much more nuanced and often brighter than our notions of them." Professor Steven Pinker, Harvard University Professor of Psychology writes, the "disconnect originates in the nature of news. News is about what happens, not what doesn't happen, so it features sudden and upsetting events like fires, plant closings, rampage shootings and shark attacks. Most positive developments are not camera-friendly, and they aren't built in a day. You never see a headline about a country that is not at war, or a city that has not been attacked by terrorists–or the fact that since yesterday, 180,000 people have escaped extreme poverty. The bad habits of media in turn ring out the worst in human cognition. Our intuitions about risk are driven not by statistics but by images and stories. People rank tornadoes (which kill dozens of Americans a year) as more dangerous than asthma (which kills thousands), presumably because tornadoes make for better television. It's easy to see how this cognitive bias–stoked by the news policy "If it bleeds, it leads"–could make people conclude the worst about where the world is heading."

Good advice is to stay aware, read, listen or watch the news maybe once or twice a day rather than every hour, and rely on other sources of information for your viewing and reading. Look for the good in what you read. Look for the opportunities.

I recommend people don't listen to the news early in the morning (unless you need to) and, in particular, people should not use the news as an alarm clock. Wake up to positive thoughts or silence. The following quotes give you more evidence and context.

I would also advise reducing your reliance on television, radio and newspaper "news." I use Google alerts and newsletter subscriptions to ensure that the positive news I am seeking gets to my inbox and to my attention.

As Raya Bidshahri, Founder & CEO of Awecademy commends, "We can't let negative headlines and the media shape our perception of ourselves as a species, and the vision we have for the future. As legendary astronomer Carl Sagan said, "For all of our failings, despite our limitations and fallibility, we humans are capable of greatness." Hollywood likes to paint disproportionately dystopian visions of the world, and while those are possible futures, we can and must also imagine a future of humanity where we live in abundance, prosperity, and transcendence. We can't expect current innovators and future generations to make this positive vision a reality if they believe our species is doomed for failure. It inspires us to continue to contribute to human progress and feel that we can push humanity forward. It's absolutely critical that our journalists cover the many challenges, threats, and issues in our world today. But just as we report the significant negative news in the world, we must also continue to highlight humanity's accomplishments. After all, how can our youth grow up believing they can have a positive impact on the world if the news is suggesting otherwise?"

Experiment: Don't listen to or read the news till you leave for work. Try this for one week. Give your family or housemates permission to share positive stories they read or hear. Let me know how the experiment goes – would you recommend it to others?

Optimism at Work

Research has found a strong link between optimism and success at work. You know people work harder towards their own goal or the team target if they expect success and to improve their lot in life.

Optimism is at the core of strategy, innovation and creativity.

In terms of sales, there are excellent studies which show optimistic salespeople and agents on average sell far more than the pessimists. There are even studies which suggest on average optimistic doctors make better diagnoses.

When you recruit, recruit optimists. What the optimist lacks in job-specific skills, they can acquire through their enthusiasm and application.

If the leading leadership firms include infectious optimism as a key trait of leadership at any level, why don't you include infectious optimism as a role requirement?

If interviewing, ask the question of the candidate for the job, what makes you optimistic? How do you infect others with your optimism? If preparing to be interviewed, prepare yourself to answer those questions.

As Sally Foley-Lewis told me, "Bringing more optimism into workplaces aligns with improving workplace cultures that lead to less staff-turnover, higher productivity and profits. Optimism can start from reframing an attitude or viewpoint from mistrust or concern to most people want to do well and most people want to get along, be engaged and be a valuable contributor."

Infectiously Optimistic Leadership

We are all called to lead from kindergarten to our death-bed.

The zeitgeist in the developed world is pessimistic and cynical. We don't need another hero, but the times call for realistic and infectiously optimistic leadership.

The best leaders are infectious optimists and lead their teams to discover greater optimism, resilience and self-mastery.

In my country, professionally and looking beyond their home-environment, Australians are increasingly pessimistic people when looking at corporations, institutions, the nation, the world and the future of work. Similar results ring true of much of the developed world.

Many economic surveys purport to measure optimism on a weekly and monthly basis. While shallow, the point I take from these surveys is that optimism is the life-blood of a growing economy. Silicon Valley and Israel thrive on the optimism of their entrepreneurs and innovators.

At the Centre for Optimism, we work around self-driven optimism, infectious optimism. A popular mantra for our participants is "The Leader looks like the person in MY mirror."

We're not talking about being a Pollyanna, although being Pollyannish does have its virtues in supporting ambition and passion. New York fashion designer Anna Sui said: "When I was a kid, my favourite movie was Pollyanna because she was the ultimate optimist. I wanted that optimism, that dreaming of the possibilities.

In our corporate and institutional work, we ask senior leaders to open up conversations right across the business on what makes the team members optimistic.

Experiment: The next meeting you lead, go round the table asking each person what makes them optimistic. Take your time, don't rush. If someone doesn't feel ready to express themselves, let them take a pass.

I recently had a businessman expressing frustration that the effect of his Monday morning pep-talks to his sales team appeared to have worn off by Monday lunchtime. I suggested he change one of his Monday morning meetings to include an opening question from each of his sales-team expressing their case for optimism. It worked! He has made it a monthly ritual at sales meetings.

So, if the leader looks like the person in your mirror, what should you do?

Ask yourself "what makes me optimistic?"

Ask your family, what makes them optimistic.

Ask your workmates, what makes them optimistic.

It can be very emotional. As you know, a good workplace can be a refuge from the problems of home, family and the rest of the world. It's worth doing. It's worth opening up a conversation on optimism at work and home. It's a good conversation!

Read: If you like, now may be a good time to turn to the section on Voices of Optimistic Leadership in Part 2 of this book. Feel free to share one of the quotes which impress you with others face-to-face or via social media.

Write: Write down your own arguments for infectiously optimistic leadership. Speak them out loud.

Optimism and Strategy

Some of the companies with the best consumer research get the optimism message. Coca Cola has included optimism in its mission statement seeking "To inspire moments of optimism and happiness through our brands and actions."

Optimism is at the core of strategy. As strategy is a large part of my work on boards and as an adviser, I have made it my business to ask others about the role of optimism in good strategy.

Allan Shaw puts it well, "Strategy is about envisioning and planning for a better future. Without optimism there is little point in planning for a better future."

How do you put this into action at work?

At the strategy and business planning level, make sure each person opens with what's going well, what makes them optimistic and what plans do they have to build a better future for the organisation and the team. If there's a strategy retreat or business retreat, make sure the facilitators are optimistic and upbeat. I have sat through too many of these sessions led by people whose business model is based on making you feel bad about how you are going as leaders, managers, innovators and the like. The message is "you're not good enough and hire me to make you better."

My view is the leader looks like the person in your mirror. Everyone leads in some element of their work and their environment.

You are good enough and can get better as can your colleagues. Optimism enlivens and impassions while pessimism paralyses.

Time Management

The eternal battle of life - work/life balance, enough time exercising, leave me time to read a book. People who look unrushed and have time to listen to you tend to be those you are drawn to.

How to find the time?

A good way to prioritise commitments was taught to me by Dadi Janki, the now 103-year-old leader of the Raj Yoga congregation, the Brahma Kumaris or BKs. Looking at my diary for the day ahead and for the period ahead, I ask

"What would God say if he was looking over my shoulder? Are there things there that I should be doing that's not there? Are there things there that are negative or a waste of good time?"

Time management is important to all of us. Again, I have adapted some advice I received from Dadi Janki and apply these rules to an invitation:

Will the commitment bring me great joy? If so, say, yes.

Will the commitment advance the cause of organisations and people I love, admire or support? If so, say, yes.

Is it something I must do? The question answers itself.

Everything else is wasted time and thought. Say no.

I allocate ten minutes each morning looking at my commitments for the day reviewing what's important and what's not, making sure I prioritise what's really important both for the day and the long-term.

Time to Think

Make sure you are not too busy. Leave some time in every day to just think - going for a walk, sitting on a bench in a park finding a quiet spot in the office. You'll find it decreases the frustration from too many things on your to do list and improves your ability to see through the static.

Which takes us on to Part 2 of this Book. Taking this book to that bench or a quiet place at work or home is a great idea.

Recently I ran a workshop in prison. One of the prisoners had been convicted of a very serious crime and I asked why he came to my session. He told me that his neighbor in the cells had come to a previous session of mine and now reads a page a day of my earlier book The Case for Optimism: The Optimists' Voices. He enjoyed his neighbor reading that page out loud.

So, whether you are serving a life-sentence or not don't feel compelled to read Part 2 cover to cover.

Read in sections, open at random and make sure to have a marker pen and markers to allow you to share the quotes that inspire or stir you with those who need some optimism and inspiration.

****

Part 2: The Optimists' Voices

Voices for the Case for Optimism

Professor Erwin Loh, Group Chief Medical Officer, St Vincent's Health Australia

"Be an optimist, and be relentless in pursuing the beacon of hope, so that you are always moving towards the light that will guide you, shine on you, and keep the shadows of darkness and despair behind you. You will also make it easier for others to find you, follow you, and be inspired by you. And by moving together in the same positive direction of hope, instead of fear, you can change the world.

Lydia Dishman, Journalist

"Optimism is our best chance to be alive instead of just live."

James Marape, Prime Minister, Papua New Guinea

"You have to be optimistic in life to achieve success. You can't be successful without optimism."

Professor Jee Hyun Kim, The Florey Institute

"Optimism is the evidence for the dreams yet to be realised."

Armando Gonzalo Alvarez Reina, Ambassador of Mexico to Indonesia

"Optimism is precisely what we need more in these times."

Anna-Marie Southern, IACCM

"Optimism is a gift; one which we are able to give to ourselves. I think it is the root of aspiration, and therefore movement and growth."

Catherine Tanna, Managing Director EnergyAustralia

"Without optimism, what are we? With optimism, we can be anything."

Dr John Miller AO FCPA FAICD, Chairman, Boardroom Management

"In all walks of life optimism endures and ensures unusual achievement."

Lynette Mayne AM, Owner + Executive Chair, Work Wear World

"Optimism is life itself – it inspires and helps us to be innovative and passionate. It creates the drive to do amazing things, to always raise the bar. Quite frankly, what would we do without it?"

Akaash Maharaj, CEO of the Global Organization of Parliamentarians Against Corruption

"Optimism is a creed for the brave. Pessimists' and cynics' certainty that nothing can be done gives them a ready excuse to do nothing and to risk nothing. By contrast, the optimist knows that better is always possible, and so he is compelled to make the effort work towards happier ends, even at the risk of disappointment."

Professor Jane Den Hollander AO, Vice-Chancellor, Deakin University

"My experience is that optimism stimulates curiosity, enables inclusion and drives a determination to do better than yesterday. Optimism is the harder journey, pessimism provides a way out and a rationale for doing nothing."

Peter Beattie AC, former Premier of Queensland

"Goodwill and optimism can change the world. It is easy to be negative but more constructive to be positive. No society grows without optimism"

Balys Stankunavicius

"In a dramatically changing world, optimism is a tonic to strengthen our challenge to contribute and construct."

Professor Lindsay Oades, Director Centre for Positive Psychology, University of Melbourne

"Anticipating the future is a central part of what it is to be human. Optimism fuels us to generate new possibilities and sustains the energy during the journey. Evidence and optimism are a potent combination."

Professor Gareth Evans AC QC, Chancellor, Australian National University

"Optimism may not be self-fulfilling, but it is self-reinforcing, just as pessimism is self-defeating. Achieving anything of lasting value in public life is difficult enough, but it is almost impossible to do so without believing that what seems to be out of reach really is achievable. I would certainly prefer to live as an optimist and often be wrong, than to live as a pessimist and always be right."

Greg Hunt, Minister for Health, Government of Australia

"Optimism is the indispensable element to success. It may not guarantee success as hard work and planning also have to be involved. But the absence of it will almost always prevent success"

Ambassador Jeff Bleich, Chair, J. William Fulbright Foreign Scholarship Board

"Optimism is knowing that, no matter what challenge we face, people acting with good will and effort can improve upon it. This isn't a dream or a wish; it is simply the story of all human progress."

Dr Suzy Green, Founder & CEO, The Positivity Institute

"Whilst the scientific community now better understands the key ingredients of a flourishing life and a flourishing world include the cultivation of gratitude, compassion and forgiveness - it is optimism and hopefulness that will help us sustain our energy and motivation to create better lives and a better world. We're not talking about unrealistic or rose coloured optimism but optimism that supports persistence in the face of negativity, resistance and adversity."

Helen Szoke, CEO at Oxfam Australia

We don't have the luxury of not being optimistic. There is too much in the world that needs optimism as the force for good and the motivation for change to make the world a better place. Yes let's analyse what is wrong and what needs to be done, but then be optimistic that we can make change. If we don't have optimism then we don't have hope!

Jane Ollis, Chair, Kent Institute of Directors

"Optimism draws you into the future. It puts you in the right space to create compelling purposeful visions, how to achieve them and then, the icing on the cake, it supplies you with the positive energy and drive you need to deliver them. Like a gentle wind pushing you from behind it steers you around obstacles as they appear in your path and keep you focussed on where you are heading."

Doron Ben-Meir, Chairman of University of Melbourne Commercial

"The case for optimism is very simple…without optimism there is no motivation and without motivation at best we exist, but we do not live! So for all those that want to live…there is no choice but optimism."

Tony Frencham, Group Managing Director, New Energy at WorleyParsons

"Humanity always provides breakthrough and uplifting moments when optimistic."

Paul Bayly, Chief Executive Officer. Virgin Islands Recovery & Development Agency

"Optimism is that special quality that gives clarity to some, comfort to others and hope to many. It is immeasurable but tangible, it is indefinable but self-evident; it is unfathomable but something we all want. It is essentially what defines us as human beings; it makes us just want to keep persevering, and it is what gets me get out of bed every morning"

Ross Dawson, Futurist, Keynote Speaker and Author

"The ONLY way we can create a better future for ourselves, our community, our organisations and humanity is to be optimistic. Optimism is absolutely not believing blindly that things will get better on their own. Optimism is believing that it is possible to create a better tomorrow if we do the right things today. Unless we have that belief we will simply give up. Only with optimism do we have a real chance of creating an amazing future for humanity."

Mauro Oretti, Vice President, SkyTeam Airline Alliance

"I find that there is a strong correlation between optimism and non-violence. Allowing ourselves to unceasingly look at the bright side of things, even when circumstances seem to suggest the opposite, drains our thought patterns from negativity – often the root cause behind violent behaviors – hence encouraging a more equipoised attitude towards the fundamentally benign nature of our universe."

Christian Duperouzel, Conscious Leadership Consultant

"In my experience, optimism is intimately associated with our spiritual awareness. In the absence of an awareness of spirit, life appears drab, lacking in substance and even threatening. Allowing the spirit in to shift these perceptions, optimism emerges from the goodness, beauty and meaning in being that we come to know characterise all forms of life at the most essential level."

David Gardner , Co-Chairman at The Motley Fool

Optimism is not just a state of mind. It's a creative force. Henry Ford famously said, "Whether you think you can, or whether you think you cannot, *you're right*."

I think you can.

Maureen Metcalf, Founder & CEO Metcalf & Associates, Author, Radio Host

"Optimism is the fuel that powers our vision and aspirations. The combination of worth vision, passion and optimism make almost anything possible. During challenging times, by surrounding ourselves with people who possess this combination we will find joy in the struggles and create a positive outcome, even if not what was originally planned."

Dr Ross Honeywill, Executive Director, Centre for Social Economics

"Optimistic people have high social intelligence - that ability to use our improbably large brains to successfully navigate complex social situations. Let's use our social intelligence to invoke a simple world view: Do not be careful what you wish for."

Professor Gabriele Oettingen, Professor of Psychology at New York University

"High optimism will predict high effort and success."

Kerry Anderson, Author of 'Entrepreneurship: It's Everybody's Business!'

"There are only two choices in life. As long as you are prepared to get out of bed every day I believe that you are an optimist. At every point in history, there is 'hardship' of all different forms. It's how you deal with it that matters. It is purely and simply up to us. No blaming anyone else!"

Dale Simpson, Executive Coach

"The Case for Optimism? Simply a positive future for all!"

Graeme Chipp, MD of the Growth Solutions Group

"Life is precious and each day worth savouring. The human spirit is the source of much optimism."

Shane Oliver, Chief Economist, AMP Capital Investors

"While it's easier and sounds more thoughtful to be a pessimist, if you want to get things done, see your living standard grow, expand your wealth and be happy it pays to be an optimist and to cheer on the optimists around you."

Cheryl Batagol, Chair, Environment Protection Authority (Victoria, Australia)

"The case for optimism centres around the human condition and the unconscious bias towards optimism of us humans but also because we have a driving need to make a difference to our bit of the world, to leave the world in a better place."

Michael Franti, Musician

"I believe the great battle that's taking place in the world isn't between left and right. It's between cynicism and optimism. There are people who believe it's possible to create a better life and a better world. When we lose that sense of optimism is when we quit, when we give up."

Tali Sharot

"Controlled experiments have shown that optimism is not only related to success, it leads to success."

Steve Wozniak "The Woz", Co-founder, Apple Computer

"H = S - F. Happiness = Smiles - Frowns. Find ways to smile and enjoy life, but don't frown. Don't argue. Don't let small things get to you. Just figure out the best path to move forward constructively. When you see pessimists, be glad that you are better with your optimism. Spread this thinking about optimism to young people. After about age 23 your personality is settled and you can't change it just with logical reasoning."

Mark Stone AM, Chief Executive of the Victorian Chamber of Commerce and Industry

"When you approach the optimism intersection always choose the green arrow and each day ask, what are the big challenges I can tackle today and how big a difference can I make!"

Tristan Russell, Adviser, City of Port Phillip

"Optimism, enthusiasm and positivity are infectious, display it, and people will always want to work with you!"

Molly Crockett, Department of Experimental Psychology, University of Oxford

"Compassion leaves its fingerprints on our beliefs about the world. We are not only optimistic about our own futures, but also the futures of those we care about. We are even optimistic about the lives of strangers, insofar as we extend our circle of concern to include distant others."

Rob Campbell, Chair of Tourism Holdings

"I see two cases for optimism. One is the essentially negative case that it is better than its opposite. The stronger case is that optimism is the force and flow of life."

Professor Elaine Fox, Rainy Brain, Sunny Brain

"Optimists tend to persevere even when it seems like the whole world is against them."

Joseph Ghaly, Leadership Coach

"Optimism is that quiet voice in our head reminding us that we are on track toward our goals. It is a refreshing consciousness that everything is going to be alright. Optimism is a state of mind and a choice. It is my choice of mindset. Is it yours? Wherever you are enroute towards your goals, whichever stop or traffic light, take a moment to be conscious of your aim. This should be an enlightening experience, refreshing your optimism about your personal motivation and original game plan. It does take energy and effort to turn on the positive or optimistic switch in our brain. That effort is well rewarded with a happier and more motivated self. And greater attraction to the people and resources who are naturally aligned with our values. Have the guts to go for it and be optimistic!"

Murli Thadani, Kiroyan Partners, Jakarta, Indonesia

"Optimism and positive energy are the platforms by which our lives are fruitfully enriched when sensibly channelised."

Prathibha Prahlad, Founder of the Delhi International Arts Festival and Bharata Natyam dancer

"One of the simplest rules of optimism - smile. Even though your heart may be sad when you smile you move energy in a positive direction."

"Optimism is to believe that the next day will be better than the last and that the next people you meet will treat you better, that no matter how hard and how tempestuous the journey, you will reach the shore intact & smiling."

Miriam Fisher, Writer and Journalist

"Our cognition is generally biased towards optimism as a survival mechanism to ensure the perpetuation of the human race. Each of us experience loss — sickness and death, relationship breakdown, financial or job loss, natural disaster — yet without this bias pushing us forward the cumulative devastation of each setback would eventually prove paralytic. But just how far we move forward depends entirely on the individual. Harnessing the power behind a negative event and guiding it in a positive direction requires the ability to identify and act on the opportunity found in loss rather than dwelling on the loss itself. So while it can be difficult to maintain a positive focus during adversity amid what can sometimes seem a cacophony of negativity, I remain very optimistic about the future. Stagnation is simply too uncomfortable an alternative and there are enough roadblocks in life that are beyond our control to allow self-imposed paralysis to set in."

Oliver Wiseman, Editor of CapX

"The case for optimism isn't based on a different estimation of the scale of the challenges we face, but a belief in our capacity to overcome them, whatever their size. Declinism of the sort that dominates in Britain and across the West is a self-fulfilling prophecy. If they want society to succeed, politicians and policymakers surely have a duty to rekindle in themselves the optimism that guides so many people's lives."

Professor Jan Blacher, University of North Carolina at Chapel Hill

"It's in the face of stress when optimism really becomes important. A mom that has a high level of optimism is going to be able to better weather stress and be better prepared mentally for the challenges ahead."

Daniel Kahneman, Author

"Optimistic people play a disproportionate role in shaping our lives. Their decisions make a difference; they are inventors, entrepreneurs, political and military leaders - not average people. They got to where they are by seeking challenges and taking risks"

Jeff Kerr-Bell

“Optimism is the only essential ingredient in all significant achievement. Apologies in advance for the auto references, but all things that are worthwhile have challenges, speed humps and barriers to overcome. It is the torque that helps drives leaders and others to overcome those barriers. Optimism, shared and well communicated, helps us believe that a vision for the future can be achieved, and compels us forward when negativity and pessimism apply the brakes. Optimism I believe is the foundation of one of my favourite quotes from Calvin Coolidge "Nothing in the world can take the place of persistence. Talent will not; nothing is more common than unsuccessful men with talent. Genius will not; unrewarded genius is almost a proverb. Education will not; the world is full of educated derelicts. Persistence and determination alone are omnipotent. The slogan "press on" has solved and always will solve the problems of the human race."

Sirajuddin Aziz

"Is optimism – a choice? Yes, it is. All of us choose to be either an optimist or a pessimist. Optimism ushers peace from within, while being the other, leads to a turbulent mind, making negative waves, for action or reaction"

General Colin Powell

“Perpetual optimism is a force multiplier"

Joe Biden, former American Vice President

"There is overwhelming reason to be optimistic."

Sir Peter Ustinov, Actor and Writer

"The point of living, and of being an optimist, is to be foolish enough to believe the best is yet to come."

Lord Blackwell

There is a strong case for optimism...Too much negativity will hold us back. It is time to put past differences behind us, be optimistic about the opportunities & work together to shape a prosperous future"

Professor the Hon Gareth Evans AC QC, Chancellor, Australian National University

"I continue to be, and describe myself, as that most unusual and perhaps implausible of creatures in this day and age – an incorrigible optimist. I am acutely conscious that always looking on the bright side lends itself to parody, as Monty Python fans will hardly need reminding. But what I offer throughout, in every one of the policy areas in which I have been immersed, are essentially two kinds of explanations for my evident naivete. The first is that, however bad things may seem to be, they often don't look quite so bad when looked at from a longer historical perspective – that's true of conflict generally, mass atrocity crimes, civil violence, major human rights violations, and certainly of poverty – and there is usually at least some objective ground for thinking there may be a way of solving, or at least containing the problem in question. Will Kim Jong-un ever really be the first to attack anyone when he knows that to be homicidal is to be suicidal? And with all the checks and balances, constraints and push backs now visibly at work against Donald Trump there seems reasonable ground for believing that the present US presidential horror- show will not careen completely out of control. My second explanation is a more basic one. I have found throughout my public life that as a practical matter, optimism is not self-fulfilling, but it is certainly self-reinforcing, just as pessimism is self-defeating. If you believe an enterprise is bound to fail, you won't even begin trying to push the envelope. Achieving anything of lasting value in public life is difficult enough, but it is almost impossible without believing that what seems out of reach really is achievable. The bottom line is simply that I would prefer to live life an optimist and periodically be proved wrong than live as a pessimist and always be right."

Albert Einstein

"Learn from yesterday, live for today, hope for tomorrow. The important thing is not to stop questioning."

"Then do not stop to think about the reasons for what you are doing, about why you are questioning. The important thing is not to stop questioning. Curiosity has its own reason for existence. One cannot help but be in awe when he contemplates the mysteries of eternity, of life, of the marvellous structure of reality. It is enough if one tries merely to comprehend a little of this mystery each day. Never lose a holy curiosity. Try not to become a man of success but rather try to become a man of value. He is considered successful in our day who gets more out of life than he puts in. But a man of value will give more than he receives."

Ameet Ranadive

"Common sense tells us that success makes people optimistic. But we have seen repeatedly that the arrow goes in the opposite direction as well. Optimistic people become successes. In school, on the playing field, and at work, the optimistic individual makes the most of his talent. And we now know why. The optimistic individual perseveres. In the face of routine setbacks, and even of major failures, he persists. When he comes to the wall at work, he keeps going, particularly at the crucial juncture when his competition is also hitting the wall and starting to wilt."

Tony Harding

"It's about attitude and state of mind! We all have challenges and obstacles to overcome. Embracing optimism and strength of will over adversity can be a game-changer for us and our colleagues - to enable us to achieve our goals in life. I recommend we embrace optimism champions and role models as part of our journey in life."

Curt Fowler, Values Driven Results

"Optimism and gratitude are the keys to a happy and successful life. They are antidotes to stress, greed and fear. Whenever you feel any of those negative emotions coming on you replace those thoughts with gratitude. Your gratitude will lead to optimism which leads to happiness which leads to success."

Syed Saeed Alam

"Optimism is the powerful elixir of engagement."

David Markus, CEO, Combo Business IT

"Choice is the luxury afforded by good planning and execution. First, have the optimism to set a worthwhile plan and then motivate yourself and others to execute in a timely manner to achieve the amazing results humanity is capable of. From this will stem life choices others only wish they could make."

Terry Williams

“My 2nd greatest fear is that I won’t achieve my potential. My greatest fear is that I already have. We must always be optimistic our best is ahead of us”

Rashidi Sumaili

"What makes an optimist is the understanding that there’s not a permanent problem or enemy in one’s life. I am an optimist and dream positively with conviction & focus on the feeling of hope"

Warren Lloyd, Director, Lower Murray Water

“As a director of a Rural Water Authority and a farmer I know the true value of optimism as a commodity. Over the years farmers have a catalogue of good and bad seasons to draw from. However it is the quest to improve and the optimism of a better year ahead that is the driving force that sustains.”

Paul Bayly, Chief Executive Officer. Virgin Islands Recovery & Development Agency

"Optimism is that special quality that gives clarity to some, comfort to others and hope to many. It is immeasurable but tangible, it is indefinable but self-evident; it is unfathomable but something we all want. It is essentially what defines us as human beings; it makes us just want to keep persevering, and it is what gets me get out of bed every morning"

Daniel McClintock, Head of Product, Vocus Communications

"The best optimist is one who sees their failures as opportunities to learn, who views an understanding of their weaknesses as a guide to their strengths, and who looks at difficult times as an occasion to identify where they need to grow, in short, an optimist is someone who strives every day to become a better version of themselves."

Brad Coughlin

"Optimism is the connective tissue between your last No and your next Yes."

Natalie Foeng, CFO, Yarra Valley Water

"Optimism is so important because it opens up new experiences and new possibilities. It is the catalyst for conquering our fears and chasing our dreams. Our future successes and our well-being depend on it."

Alex Steffen, Futurist

"I think, now more than ever, choosing and voicing optimism is a powerful political action."

Kate Ashmor, Lawyer

"Optimism brings with it a level of happiness and belonging that negativity and pessimism never can. Looking on the bright side, looking ahead, brings people together, creates a cohesiveness that is infectious."

Jennifer Jarrard, IACCM

O Openness Opportunity
P Passion Positivity
T Thinking
I Interactions with Inspiring People
M Mindset
I Interrelationships
S Service
T Teamwork
I Innovation
C Creativity & Collaboration

OECD Study on Social and Emotional Skills

"Emotional stability skills are found to be the most predictive of mental health. Optimism has the highest relation to life satisfaction scores"

Dona Tantirimudalige, Yarra Valley Water

"Conscious, deliberate optimism, particularly in the face of what might feel like overwhelming adversity, is crucial to success.

What do I mean by that?

Sometimes there are no easy paths to follow. Sometimes there are no easy options. In these situations in particular, if we are to succeed in any measure, it is critical that we step into the challenges we face with determination, grit, drive, and optimism.

Not blind optimism – but deliberate optimism embraced in the full and conscious knowledge of the facts and challenges we face. It is the only way we can succeed in these situations."

Tracey Slatter, MD. Barwon Water

"More than ever, we need optimism - not hope - but determination and endeavour to lead through the complex challenges we face and achieve the remarkable"

World Bank President Jim Yong Kim

"For me optimism is a moral choice"

James Macmillan, Director at PwC Australia

"I truly believe there is no motion without emotion and that 'I live what I believe I am'. That is, where my focus goes my energy will flow. Therefore, I believe in being an optimistic leader focussed on positive outcomes, clear on purpose and pumped about why those outcomes matter. From there results will always follow."

Helen Clark, Former Prime Minister of New Zealand

"It's always best to keep an optimistic outlook. Because pessimism doesn't get you anywhere"

Diann Rodgers-Healey, Director, Australian Centre for Leadership for Women

"Optimism is believing in the greatness of humanity and its potential to reach heights for the greater good. It is knowing that one has endless inner resources that one can draw upon when needed to transform barriers. My case for optimism is linked to purpose and integrity as each of the three are intertwined in clarifying and persisting a way forward."

Rose Jost, Wellbeing Coach

"Optimism is a form of cognitive flexibility, whereby the individual, regardless of their past or current circumstances, is able to see the valley beyond the mountain. Optimists envisage potential in themselves and those around them, pivot around challenge and cultivate an attitude of perseverance. Optimism is deeply human; harnessing collaboration, mobilisation and disruption while acknowledging the full spectrum of experience and emotion. Optimism is not a zero-sum game; it does not require the absence of fear, failure, setbacks or obstacles, rather an agile mindset and a heart full of hope."

Rod Snodgrass

"Regarding optimism and how I feel about the world and things I cannot go past this quote from Virgil.

"They can because they think they can"

I simply believe everything can and will be better. The gap between that and now is belief and courage and a smattering of good human values. There is nothing you can do about yesterday other than learn from it. It has gone. There is only today and tomorrow"

Major General Vinod Saighal

"Optimism is the only antidote to the depression, dejection and hopelessness that has enmeshed large portions of the globe due to poverty and exacerbated by wars that keep recurring somewhere or the other."

Professor Madhu Bhaskaran, RMIT

"Optimism is looking for rainbows when it rains and looking for stars when it is dark."

Pamela Jabbour , founder and CEO of the Total Image Group

"I believe positivity is a superpower and optimism is the magic dust that helps push you through. Life is what you make it. In business and in life we all have good days, bad days, overwhelming days and days where our whole world gets thrown upside down. In leadership, the trials and tribulations of each day and minute can be hard to navigate. While the challenges can vary, every challenge brings with it a need to keep going, push through and not give up. Being positive and optimistic sets me up to deal with challenges as they arise clearly and confidently."

Krystian Seibert, Centre for Social Impact, Swinburne University.

"Social impact is all about optimism. Whether we're trying to understand a complex problem, to shape public policy, to enhance the effectiveness of our charities or grow philanthropy - it's all driven by a firm belief that by working together as a community, we can change our society for the better. We need to be optimists to keep our minds open to new perspectives and ideas, and to keep on striving even when we face a setback."

Stan Shih and Jon Gordon (on separate occasions)

"Optimism is a competitive advantage"

Optimists on their Optimism

Frances Adamson, Secretary, Australian Department of Foreign Affairs and Trade

"My Aunt Nancy, now in her nineties, recently wrote to one of our children in hospital: "My prayer for you is to be optimistic. Remember - dark clouds pass and blue skies follow." That's true in life, but in international relations optimism needs to be harnessed to policy development, advocacy, consensus building and effective implementation in order to produce outcomes which support peace and prosperity. Blue skies are infinitely preferable to dark clouds and that is why I am, personally and professionally, an active optimist!"

Professor David Bowtell, Ovarian Cancer Research

"Who wouldn't be optimistic! In 100 years we have progressed from the first identification of distant galaxies and the concept of relativity, to being able to detect neutron stars colliding and disrupting the fabric space, using detectors of extraordinary precision. A little over 50 years has passed since the structure of DNA was first described and now we can read and interpret the genomes of any organism on Earth in just a few hours. We have become a super organism, where the components – us – have become connected with increasing speed and inclusion; first by voice, then print, and now the internet. When harnessed for good, the possibilities for humanity as a collective are unimaginable."

Johan Norberg, Author, 'Progress: Ten Reasons to Look Forward to the Future'

I am not an optimist because mankind just happen to be lucky, by coincidence, but because we have built a social and political infrastructure for luck. The more eyeballs that look at problems, and the more brains that can think about how to solve them, the more problems will be solved. And in an open world, with more people than ever, living longer than ever, with more access to knowledge and with more freedom to communicate, collaborate and trade than ever, we have in effect created the biggest problem-solving machine the world has ever seen.

Dr Robyn Stokes

"Optimism is the only mindset. It has urged us to fly into the sky and beyond, see a tiny window of time or space to make a difference, seize it, fail and try again - in our hearts we know we can be 'third or fourth time lucky'. Inspiration comes from big and small things and just taking a few vital minutes to consider what's missing in the mundane. Inspiration comes from those before us and after us, from words and action and from what is left unsaid or undone. It is young people cleaning up our oceans patch by patch, building new communities, changing the workplace and sweating less small stuff. It is old people telling stories of what they have conquered and all of us taking the time once in a while 'to pick up our own opportunities and turn them over like seashells to listen and really hear the sea'."

Chris Reddy, Leadership Coach

"What makes me optimistic? It's pretty simple. It's all about appreciating the small things, accepting the setbacks, grasping opportunities and being grateful for the family and friends in my life."

Professor Paul Mazerolle, President, University of New Brunswick

"Optimism for the future is the recognition that our progress as a global community requires human ingenuity, creativity, innovation, knowledge, partnerships, tolerance and values. Progress is not inevitable. It requires commitment, actions over words, good deeds over promises, as well as proactive responses and co-active efforts. Despite the challenges and setbacks across the 20 century, the achievements over the past hundred years are remarkable. I am optimistic for the future because of my fundamental belief in the skills, values, and commitment of people to make a difference for the world, supported by the wider community in enacting or supplying resources and conditions to enable human flourishing to endure. Long may it continue!"

Tracy McLeod Howe, CEO, NSW Council of Social Service

"Persistent optimism is a must in my line of work. It's what drives a good advocate. Optimism that we can make our world better, optimism that others will join our drive for change, optimism that each of us has the power to make a difference. And you never know when that optimism will have a breakthrough. Give everything a try once, I say. Be comfortable with failing. Better to say, "ok, that didn't work – what's next," than to be constantly saying, "that won't work.""

Fabian Dattner, Leadership Expert

"Ultimately optimism is founded on the premise that something better is possible and that there is always a better way to look at life and see options, at least one of which sparkles. Victor Frankl, the author of *'Man's Search for Meaning'*, thought it was because there was something yet to be done in life and this belief enabled people to survive in the most awful of places. For myself I just can't imagine not trying to build a better world, doing my bit to sow the seeds of possibility. So at heart I am optimistic... or possibly mad! I prefer the former."

John Stanhope, Chancellor, Deakin University

"I am extremely optimistic about our future because the creativity of people always finds a way to solve problems and change things for the better. History shows that while many problems seem insurmountable optimistic creative people make the difference. New jobs will be created, new industries will emerge and an exciting new future will continue to evolve"

Andrew Liveris, Chair, The Dow Chemical Company

"In many cases, globalization and capitalism has been a force for good. At the same time, a substantial part of humanity has been left behind by growth that has been uneven and inequitable, creating a global environment marked by anger, violence, inequality, and divisiveness. Despite all of this, I remain as optimistic as ever. Today's world is abundant with opportunity to collaborate in new ways, creating positive change and solutions that protect the planet and provide hope to millions of people who feel that the world has forgotten them. To use a math metaphor, we can choose to live on the numerator, a person who adds to and multiplies the good versus living on the denominator as someone who subtracts, or worse, divides. If we embrace this opportunity and collaborate to solve some of the biggest challenges facing society, we truly can positively impact the lives of billions of people, making life better for themselves, their loved ones, and the communities around them."

Anne Crawford, Healthcare Consultant and Philanthropist

"I am very optimistic for our future. Worldwide we are seeing an improvement in people's health. Longer lifespans and more equity in wealth. The near eradication of polio is very exciting. But we still have human rights issues we need to work on. But we are discussing these issues more widely."

Adam Bowcutt, Psychologist

"I am very optimistic and excited about the future. The opportunities that will be created as a result of technology and its integration into everyday life will be great. Barriers to entry and opportunity have been reduced due to easy access to the internet and online communities. The basis for my answer is from vision and logic and a healthy, non-fearful approach. The natural human ability to learn and adapt quickly will be valuable. Will there be big challenges? Yes. Bring on these challenges!"

Rose Godde, Arts Leader

I am optimistic for the future because: At the heart we humans are a solutions driven species; Empathy is the core driver for human survival; and, each generation sees the world afresh calling out the past generation's failures and successes within the context of their own changing times.

Christiana Figueres,

"I am a stubborn optimist. Nothing gets done without optimism. Have you known a breakthrough that started with pessimistic thoughts about its potential? But our optimism cannot be naïve and ignorant: We must acknowledge the many challenges along the way, not as road blockers, but as challenging invitations to find a better path."

Dr Elliot F Eisenberg, President and Chief Economist, GraphsandLaughs, LLC

"While many are pessimistic about the future, reality suggests that optimism is most appropriate. We are living longer, safer and better lives than ever before. Poverty, while still a problem, is less of a problem than ever before. Diseases that killed millions are being eradicated. And, the percentage of the global population that live in nations that are democratic is near an all-time high. This is a great time to be alive and I look forward to the medical and technological breakthroughs that are around the corner. People do great things every day."

Tenzing Lamsang

"Optimism? The broad sweep of history shows we are more prosperous, peaceful and equal than at any time in history. Yes, we have our issues (the biggest one is climate change) but humanity is getting better"

Rick Wartzman, Drucker Institute

"Being optimistic doesn't mean ignoring the many difficult challenges that society is up against. It means facing them head on while believing, deep down, that we have the capacity and compassion to take on these challenges and ultimately lick them. It means believing in our collective ability to triumph over adversity."

Kerry Vincent, Sugar Art Queen and Television Compere

"Conventional wisdom is that the world is cloaked in clouds of fear, inequity, discrimination violence and poverty. No matter how optimistic one can be these things lurk in the background screaming to be fixed. Generations of prejudice and cultural misbehavior are beginning to break down little by little as new age optimists bite the bullet and address issues head on. I have great faith in the youth of the world I expect them to push back and bury the mistakes of the past. For me, I have always been an optimist and a risk taker, how else could I have found my way from the red dirt in Australia to a career that I love in the US, and to be in a position to help others achieve their dreams."

Peter Schechter, Altamar: A Foreign Affairs Podcast.

"It's easy to be a pessimist in this world. Too easy to forget the spreading prosperity of formerly poor countries. Too easy to overlook that more people are eating better than ever before. That education is more widely available. And disease more easily curable across countries. So, as we read headlines about xenophobia, violence, refugees and discontent, let's not forget that there is not only a case for optimism. There is a cause for optimism."

Juliet Bourke, Deloitte

"I don't know why I am an optimist, but clearly I am. It could stem from an innate nature or how I have been nurtured, or perhaps both? What I do know is that I have an inner belief in the goodness of other people, and I think that is intertwined with my optimistic outlook. I heard someone say recently 'There are a lot of reasons to be cynical, but we don't have time. All I see is potential to improve'. I can relate to those sentiments. It's not that I don't apply a lens of critical analysis – I do – but I have an unshakeable faith that ultimately things will work out and bad times are temporary."

Stephanus Cecil Barnard, University of Southern Queensland

"I am deeply optimistic. I see the calamity in world politics and our elected representatives as the jump start we needed to know we need to care for ourselves. Too many people believe it is the government's job, and therefore never excel or push their boundaries (the one problem with rich countries); I also believe robotics and artificial intelligence will change the world in a dramatic manner. I see our biggest challenge will be ongoing consumption for the sake of want and not need."

Nick Smit, International Affairs Expert

"I am optimistic for the future of the world's population as rising education standards, nutrition, disease control, birth control and employment, particularly in hitherto impoverished regions, are leading to a better life for more people. I am worried by the tendency of many in the developed world to want everything to stay the way it is now, e.g. to stop replacing native growth with rural development and rural by urban development. People seem to be happy live on cleared bushland but refuse to allow anyone else to clear bushland to live on. A major challenge for leaders of the future is to find the right balance between development and conservation which will be key to improving global living standards and thus, happiness. Too many in the developed world are fearful of change at a time when the rate of change, particularly in the case of technological change, is accelerating rapidly."

Mike McRoberts, News Anchor at TV3, New Zealand

"Optimism is having faith in the destination when you have no idea how you are going to get there. I believe if you travel your journey in an optimistic way you can overcome any obstacle."

Dena Schusterman

"I am optimistic about our future because despite so much darkness there are still those who choose to illuminate our world by being lamplighters, igniting one soul at a time."

Paul Lehmann, Australian Ambassador

"We live in an imperfect world, but when you meet as many talented, generous and resilient people as I do every day, the case for optimism very often makes itself."

Porendra Pratap

"Gratitude for what nature has given me makes me optimistic. Very simple good things happening to me in my daily journey of life make me happy and grateful and optimistic."

Christine Hammett

"I am always optimistic and have a positive attitude. If you didn't what's the point of living. Life is a challenge and you have your up moments and down moments but you keep on going."

Bob Brown, former Leader of the Australian Greens

"Optimism, like pessimism, feeds on itself. In my earlier years I spent a decade or more deeply pessimistic and depressed. Even though it was a reasonable reaction to the way the human world malfunctions, it wasn't an enjoyable way to live. These days I am an optimist and I like it. It is also a reasonable option because optimism is a key ingredient for any successful human endeavour -and isn't keeping earth viable the greatest endeavour we can never undertake?"

Dr Melissa Geraghty

"What makes me optimistic is knowing that there is an ebb and flow in life, nothing is permanent. There is comfort in that."

Michael McCormack, Deputy Prime Minister of Australia

"Serving the people living in the regions is what keeps me optimistic, even in the toughest of days. These people have put their trust in me to fight and deliver for our local communities, and I will always speak up for them loudly."

Leonie Hemingway

"As a woman and a mother, with no tertiary education and entering politics at middle age, to the right of the political aisle, Optimism was about the best ally I had. It's really just another word for belief."

Helen Keller, Author

"Although the world is full of suffering, it is full also of the overcoming of it. My optimism, then, does not rest on the absence of evil, but on a glad belief in the preponderance of good and a willing effort always to cooperate with the good, that it may prevail. I try to increase the power God has given me to see the best in everything and everyone and make that Best a part of my life."

Robert Safian, Editor in Chief, Fast Company

"I am a believer in the power of optimism, the drive and creativity that possibility can engender. I believe in it not the way a child would, but knowing full well the perils and pitfalls that the world can put in your path. Today there is much to be anxious about when we get up each day. Uncertainty reigns as rapid change disrupts expectations and social norms. Global leadership is fractured and economic conditions fluctuate widely. Specters loom, from climate change to cyberterrorism. The relentless pace can make you want to curl up in a corner, wary of what might come next. Or you can stare unblinkingly at this time of chaos and dig into the difficult work of building a better tomorrow."

Chuck Swindoll, Insight for Living Ministries

"When you have vision it affects your attitude. Your attitude is optimistic rather than pessimistic. Your attitude stays positive rather than negative. Not foolishly positive, as though in fantasy, for you are reading God into your circumstances. So when a situation comes that cuts your feet out from under you, you don't throw up your arms and panic. You don't give up. Instead, you say, "Lord, this is Your moment. This is where You take charge. You're in this."

Julie Hryniewicz, Author

"I choose optimism because I have found that when my mind is set in the right direction, when I am grateful, when I am appreciative and when I am seeking the positive perspective, bright side or blessings in all situations, I am more likely to attract positive things, opportunities and situations into my reality"

Christina Pagano, Pagano and Company Public Relations

"I do remain confident in the basic goodness of the citizens of the world, most of whom wake up in the morning, and regardless of where they live or under what circumstances, aim to do the best they can in the course of the day. And in many cases, execute remarkable acts of kindness. I see that in New York City every day."

Bill Ghormley, Xconomy

"The motto for the city of St. Andrews: Dum Spiro, Spero = while I breathe, I hope. This is the founding principle of my optimism -- while we live, we can always make life better. While this comes from Scotland, this sentiment carries across the globe, especially relevant to Australia, Europe, and the USA, where great melting pots of migrants have redefined society -- and where eternal values need to be embraced."

Chris Dollar

"Whether they own it or not, anyone who fishes is an optimist. Same goes for crabbers and hunters. No doubt each of us possess varying degrees of this trait, but you must be somewhere on that spectrum that fuses hope with confidence in pursuit of what ultimately is a wild thing."

Louise McGrath, Global Business Expert

"The Case for Optimism? I was thinking about this question when I was at a meeting with Australia's Trade Negotiators at DFAT. Can you get any more optimistic than negotiating trade deals for future exports? I am very optimistic for the future as I am fortunate to be surrounded by Australian manufacturers who are standing up to take on the world, exporters who are launching into new markets, and all the lovely and optimistic people who make up the ecosystem of support for Australian industry. I am also very fortunate to meet leaders and business people from across Asia pacific. When you think about where countries like Vietnam and South Korea have come from and where they are heading, you can't be anything but optimistic."

Dr Marija Maher, The University of Melbourne

"Anyone can become an optimist. In my experience optimism is not synonymous with luck, but using every opportunity and trying, and failing, and trying some more. Like you, I am dismayed about a lack of recognition of the environment in Australia, environment that allows people to have a go. And as an 18-year-old refugee who came to Australia without a word of English and on my own, I know just how lucky this country is. More importantly, I recognise that it took more than luck for me to feel optimistic as a leader and as an Australian. It took determination, hard work, persistence and perseverance. For me, optimism – in leadership and in life – is knowing that you can try at anything, and if it doesn't work you can pick yourself up and try again."

Andrew Macleod, Global Australian Humanitarian

"The greatest gift being an aid worker in disaster and conflict zones has given me, is a deeper understanding how lucky we are to have the small things. Drinking water from the tap, crossings on roads, food in supermarkets, and the ability to sit at the MCG surrounded by people passionately supporting opposing teams in a game, but to do so peacefully. With this great good fortune as our base, imagine all that we can achieve when we decide we wish to."

Josie McLean, Leadership Coach

"I am an optimist and global dynamics such as population growth, continuous economic growth, declining quantity and quality of arable land, declining fish stocks etc. etc. etc. mean that humanity will 'go through the fire ' yet. As we do, we can recall how crisis has drawn out the best in us on many occasions. Drawn out our compassion and willingness to contribute to a greater, common good. Reflect on some irrigators on the River Murray during the drought and how some contributed their water allocations to the environment. Think of the Victorian bushfires etc. Humans also have a great capacity for novelty and creativity. I think we have displayed less capacity for thinking through unintended consequences before we follow through in some major technological advances. Thinking of nuclear capacity here. And also wondering if we have thought through artificial intelligence well enough yet. On one hand a brilliant innovation with capacity for widening social divides if used poorly. A time of paradoxes perhaps...Have we asked and answered the questions 'what is it to be human?' And 'how do we really want to live?' Just because we can do something doesn't mean we should - and yet it seems human arrogance is strong."

Teresa Engelhard

"What makes me optimistic today? I like to zoom out and look at where we've come from, and it's really hard not to be optimistic when you do that. Particularly I think, being a female in our society, you just have to zoom out a little bit - a hundred years - and you can see a huge amount of progress. Zoom out even further, and you can see the progress of mankind, going from our violent, alpha primate programming to using our intellect to develop an ability to evolve ourselves. We, speaking broadly about mankind, have used our own thinking to design transcended capability, shifting our evolutionary path from biological molecules to thought processes. And so I think our challenge is continuing to shift in that positive direction and history has proven that it's at least possible, if not inevitable."

President Barack Obama

"We have to reject the notion that we're suddenly gripped by forces that we cannot control. We've got to embrace the longer and more optimistic view of history and the part that we play in it. If you are skeptical of such optimism, I will say something that may sound controversial. I used to say this to my staff in the White House, young interns who would come in, any group of young people that I met with, and that is that by just about every measure, America is better, and the world is better, than it was 50 years ago, 30 years ago, or even 10 years ago."

Anne Crawford, Author and Healthcare Consultant

"I am very optimistic for our future. Worldwide we are seeing an improvement in people's health. Longer lifespans and more equity in wealth. The near eradication of polio is very exciting. But we still have human rights issues we need to work on. But we are discussing these issues more widely. In Australia we are seeing improvements in our First people's lifespans, we are working on an enormous social improvement through the disability insurance scheme, we are more openly discussing human rights issues such as domestic violence, suicide prevention, mental health issues, LGBQTI issues and homelessness to name a few. These discussions are leading to activities that are supportive and directed. I am excited by this and feel we are becoming a more aware and caring society as a result. I see improvements everywhere. There is still much more to do but the work is being done."

Professor Dimity Dornan, Executive Director, Hear & Say

"I have been blown away by the amazing results obtained by young children using a combination of the Australian-invented bionic ear combined with powerful listening-brain learning. I am now totally optimistic about the possibilities for treating previously untreatable medical conditions successfully with other emerging bionics technologies like the bionic eye, heart, limbs, organs and brains. Trying to analyse this optimism has led me to believe it is a feeling of hope mixed with a firm belief in a strong possibility of success! Optimism is an exhilarating motivator, a vigorous call for personal action and a strength in time of challenge. It is indeed the "wind beneath my wings" as I actively work towards accelerating the industry."

Madeleine Albright, former USA Secretary of State

"I Am an Optimist Who Worries A Lot"

Strobe Talbott, Brookings Institution

"I would without shame confess to being an optimist. Little by little, with obvious setbacks and mistakes and follies, we the human race, are going to not just make it, but make it better."

Peter Saul, Futurist

"I think globalised trade is a major driver of my own optimism as, to put it simply, I don't think countries bomb their customers. I agree with the comment by Peter Whiting that our political leadership never talks about a long term, positive vision for Australia and its place in the world - the common good. Our politicians fight skirmishes over gay marriage, who should build our submarines, what the tax rate should be, etc. These debates are never argued within the context of where we all wish to go as a nation. Ideally there should be a lot of bipartisanship around where we want the nation to be in 25 years time. Perhaps bipartisanship is anathema to the Westminster system of government. If so we should be reinventing government for the 21st century. I often fear that the Westminster system has no mechanism within it for its continual renewal as times change."

Kevin Kelly

"Over the long term, the future is decided by optimists"

Bob White, CEO at EB2BCOM

“One of my favourite books of all time is Matt Ridley's "The Rational Optimist", and I have recently read it yet again. The title says it all - I like to think that rationalism and optimism are two of my guiding principles. I believe that it should be required reading for leaders, and particularly parents, teachers, politicians, academics and business people. Add to this a vision for the country's future and a path to get there and it covers most of the key requirements for political leadership. Unfortunately I see little of this in our current crop.”

Arun Bhuta, Director, Slim Money

“I am perpetual optimist. As I believe in what I give is what I will get.”

Patrick Gleeson

“I am generally an optimistic person. Some will be more optimistic than me, but on the whole I prefer to look at things optimistically. I believe we will eventually learn from past mistakes and past adversity. In some respects humans will get to a point where they will search again for simple values and try and find some commonality. I guess we do go through these cycles. Will advancements happen? Yes, because we are all still evolving and a work in progress. Humans still have the capacity for wonderment and to learn. What we have to be aware of though, is not losing the connection to our base, to our surroundings and to nature and nurture. Sounds airy, fairy, but that is what can keep us grounded.”

Jodie Ginsberg, Chief Executive, Index on Censorship.

"In a world in which it's easy to feel bombarded by the negative, I am constantly uplifted by the stories of those striving to make the world a better place - through small acts of kindness and grand acts of sacrifice. Human beings are essentially good. Knowing that is enough to champion the case for optimism."

Michelle A. Waters

"What makes me optimistic is the capacity for people to love, learn and change. There is so much goodness inside everyone if we choose to see it, get out of our head and become still on the inside"

Mark Bailey, Goulburn Valley Water

"I feel optimistic because of mankind's continual desire to learn and challenge. It happens throughout our societies. Investigators want to know why, how and if it can be done better. Scientists and engineers are tremendous examples of this thirst"

Michelle Mannering

"I'm optimistic when I think about the good in others. Strive to see the positives. Instead of seeing everything as an obstacle, I see things as challenges. Take that challenge and believe you can create real change."

Michael Rowland, Presenter, ABC TV Breakfast News

"I'm optimistic because it beats the alternative! I have always taken a glass-half-full approach to life because there is no problem that can't be solved with a dose of positivity and a spirit of cooperation."

Kyle Farris, Leadership Development

"Focusing on the negative isn't difficult. We're hardwired to identify threats in our environment and allow them to shape our narrative. For some, it can bury us. It torments our self-perception, our relationships, and our effectiveness. It takes a strong force of will to balance the acknowledgement of a threat with sincere optimism. In that balance, we say, "My environment does not define me; I define my environment." Optimism, therefore, is not a whimsical notion of ignorance; it is a devotion to be an agent of change in an otherwise entropic world of thought."

Anthony Chiminello

"Optimism is a choice I make to see the best in people circumstances and events which in turn manifests into greater opportunities."

Riva Levinson

"I am an optimist because life has taught me to follow my heart and not to fear being misunderstood. I have come to see that certainty is a luxury and destiny a journey that reveals itself with time. It's easy to stray off course, to doubt and lose faith. To see compromise as surrender. To feel judged, isolated, even abandoned. But there is always something to hold on to the belief that things will get better. I have come to appreciate that we need people to guide us, those we admire, those we believe in - the heroes that we choose."

Rich Tehrani, Futurist

“I am optimistic because technology has improved the lives of billions and given them more for less. More food, better communication, better shelter, better entertainment and far greater earning power.”

Michael Stallard

“I believe people can work together to make the future brighter. Not everything is in our control, certainly, but time and again throughout history optimistic people have pulled together and persevered to overcome obstacles and achieve great ends."

Wendy Scaife

"What makes me optimistic? I always think the human spirit is like a Roly Poly Clown who gets knocked down but ends up upright again. The only way is up!"

Cissy White

"Open not broken is my motto. Optimism isn't false perk or cheer. It's the beauty of truth-telling, honesty, and sharing what we've learned climbing mountains, knowing we've cleared some way for those who follow."

Melinda Stuart-Adams

"For me, optimism gives the inner confidence that everything will be alright in the end. It is this confidence that drives the motivation and energy to not always accept the status quo."

Luke Bayley, Bush Heritage Australia

"What makes me optimistic is that there are so many beautiful places, moments, and people. We need to actively gravitate and invest our time and energy into these wild, creative and special places."

Bishop Philip Huggins

"What makes me optimistic is that if we are attentive to what we let ourselves think about, it will shape the words that we use so they'll all be poetry, and our actions will create beauty, they will be truthful, and they will be kind"

Jack Zenger, CEO of Zenger | Folkman

"In a few days I'll turn 86, and I am absolutely convinced that the best days of my life are ahead of me and not behind me."

Jarrod McLauchlan

"People can't control everything that happens to them and around them. We, the optimists, have powers of self-control to respond for the better with a positive mental state. Optimism is a choice which I make and commend."

Bill Gates

"Being an optimist doesn't mean you ignore tragedy and injustice. It means you're inspired to look for people making progress on those fronts, and to help spread that progress more widely. If you're shocked by the idea of millions of children dying, you ask: Who is good at saving kids, and how can we help them do more? This is essentially why Melinda and I started our foundation."

Andrew Stoner, Former Deputy Premier NSW

"I know I am blessed to be an optimist. My lofty goals in life have been shaped by optimism, it lifts me off the canvas when the inevitable hard knocks come, and it enables me to experience happiness in the little things in life."

Andrea Jones

"Optimism is a choice and I like feeling good. In every thought or decision, we have the opportunity to choose the light or the dark. Why not choose the one that feels good?"

Richard Hayward, Australian Housing and Urban Research Institute

"Despite doom and gloom evidenced in the mainstream media and the apparent lack of progress on democratic and political issues, there is a real sense that individuals and organisations have the capacity to make a difference and to create change that will drive progress forward."

The Honourable Lindsay Tanner

"The last few decades have seen astonishing progress on many fronts around the world. While we still face many challenges - including overwhelming threats like climate change - any pessimism regarding the twenty-first century is easily cured by examining the twentieth".

Sarah Elaklouk, University of Queensland

"Democracy makes me optimistic and free speech makes me optimistic amongst other things!'

Gay Veale, US Air Force Chief Master Sergeant

"I'm an eternal optimist, and I believe in the power of positivity. Stay focused on the task at hand and realize you're working toward something bigger than yourself. Stay positive."

Diksha Dutta

"Optimism is hard-work, but it is also magic. I made it a habit. Soon there were a series of events that made me believe that magic happens to those who combine hard work with kindness, positivity and optimism."

Greg Lopez, Murdoch University

"It was the best of times,
it was the worst of times,
it was the age of wisdom,
it was the age of foolishness,
it was the epoch of belief,
it was the epoch of incredulity,
it was the season of Light,
it was the season of Darkness,
it was the spring of hope,
it was the winter of despair ....

All generations can see different realities. It is optimism that enables each generation to preserve and go on to greater things."

Steve Linde, editor-in-chief of The Jerusalem Report

"Good stories make me optimistic! Elie Wiesel was once asked why God created human beings. "Because He loves a good story."

Richard Hames, Futurist

"In an age of systemic collapse, environmental breakdown, divisive social media and fear-driven government policies, optimism is an act of rebellion."

James Pearson, CEO Australian Chamber of Commerce

"What makes me an optimist is because I believe in the future. And to believe in the future means that you are always ready to do things today that will make life better, for yourself and for your family and for your community, tomorrow"

Andi Roberts, Leadership Coach

"What makes me optimistic is our capacity for compassion and reflection alongside our capability to change our way of being."

Scott Tindle

"I'm optimistic because it gives my brain a competitive advantage and allows me to move in the world worrying about things I can control rather than those I can not."

Sarvesh Shashi, Yogi

"The fact that I breathe makes me optimistic."

Denise Hearn, Author

"I am optimistic because every day, thousands of humans help me live my life - both directly and indirectly. From the farmer who harvested coffee beans to the manufacturer who crafted my coffee mug & the restaurateur who seats me in her establishment"

John Lavis

"What makes me optimistic?
Young children and octogenarians
Songwriters and their songs
Scientists and their plans
Bright eyes and a knowing smile
Quiet people laughing together"

Craig Conte, Elevate Services

"I am optimistic because no matter what the political winds are, more and more people are being connected. The more we know, the more we learn, the more we understand, and less and less we are the 'other'."

Vibeke Koushede

"What makes me optimistic is knowing that even a single person can make a marked positive difference in the world and that people all over the world do so every day."

Runa Bouius

"What makes me optimistic is the spark of life-force we all have inside ourselves - the connection to our inner guidance system and to the source that makes anything possible."

Ian Opperman, NSW Chief Data Scientist

"I am optimistic because every day brings new challenges and conquering these challenges is the stuff of life."

Brian Tuohy

"I am optimistic because I believe that I haven't had my best day yet, but I have the potential to do so, and even if today is fantastic, imagine how much better my best day will be when it happens."

Nikki Hutley, Economist, Deloitte Access Economics

"I have to confess I'm not always optimistic. But it's often at the bleakest of times that we see the best of humanity. In the end, I think it's seeing others striving to make the world a better place, inch by inch, that keeps me optimistic and motivated."

Craig Rispin, Futurist

"I'm an optimist because I believe in the future!"

Eloise Grace, Advisory Committee, Centre for Optimism

"Optimism is making the most of every day - be it during work, social catch ups or family time. It's also seeing the beauty all around you, which is everywhere if you take the time to look."

Marian Salema

“What makes me optimistic is seeing people coming together and collaborating to solve the world's most pressing problems. Optimism is radical. It is the hard choice, the brave choice. It is about believing that the future can be better than the present.”

Alvin Foo, MD, Reprise Digital

"Optimism is the magic that keeps everything going. It helps us to see opportunities in every problem!"

Lisa Dwyer, Dairy Farmer

"No matter how challenging farming can sometimes be, the first-born calf for the season never fails to bring a renewed sense of optimism for the year ahead!"

John Salter, Disaster Resiliance Consultant

"What makes me optimistic? That humans can exercise free will guided by purpose. History is threaded with struggles - at all levels, from individuals to global efforts - to achieve. That freedom often generates a struggle between opposites, but that is the dialectic we all move forward with."

Richard Neumann, Australian Diplomat

"That we are better off as a race than we have ever been and we have a strong consensus and commitment to address remaining pockets of poverty and starvation, including among the world's First Nations that remain the most disadvantaged globally, gives me great cause for optimism."

David Thomas, Australian China Expert

"I'm an optimist. Always have been. I like to take people with me on the journey without being too constrained by the potential for failure. There are plenty of people around to show you the potholes"

Dr Paul Zeitz, Co-Founder of SDG Compacts

"An alchemy of clear-eyed optimism mixed with courage is what fuels my drive to pursue justice for all relentlessly, no matter the odds"

Sally Hughes, CEO of The International Association for Contract & Commercial Management (IACCM)

"What makes me optimistic is an innate desire to be happy. And I take personal responsibility for being a happy and positive person - for seeing the opportunities and overcoming challenges - not giving up. I guess I'm ambitious too and I'm sure ambition requires optimism."

Professor Tim Cummins, President, IACCM

"I am optimistic because of the past. Looking back over history, humanity has faced many challenges and taken many wrong turns, yet its progress in raising the quality of life has been nothing short of remarkable."

Paul Dorrington, Energy and Extracts

"Optimism is the ability to face any situation, believe in yourself that you can find a solution to any problem that you will encounter on your journey. As a scientist and engineer however, there is a caution to go with optimism - optimism can blind those who have not prepared or have not sought the very best minds and information currently available or are not fully aware of what has gone before them, so that they can truly apply the facts and knowledge to improve the future. You must first acknowledge the problem, understand it and then seek to solve it.

I remain optimistic that the tide is turning and that the world will look at the past, learn from it and act rapidly – I remain optimistic that we will realise that balance and sustainable equilibrium are more important than growth, that we will reduce the global population to a sustainable level, we will manage and recycle our resources before they are exhausted, we will eliminate pollution of our environment and treasure biodiversity but above all .... provide knowledge and education to all people to be able to understand, act with rigour, confidence and be optimistic for themselves, to have respect for all life on this planet (and perhaps others one day). Our failed societies in the past have crumbled due to either ideological, political or economic folly, the consumption or destruction of all the resources within their accessible environment or because of an adverse environmental condition – we are no longer geographically isolated in this, we are capable of doing this to the entire world.

If we achieve the goals I have mentioned, then I believe the problems we see as tragic can be prevented – we have the means and technology today to globally provide, not just our basic needs - of housing, safety, food, water, sanitation, health but also deliver on our creative wants and needs for the future and have a healthy, beautiful environment in which to live. I am optimistic that we will not fear the unknown but will embrace it, understand it, protect what is truly important, find balance, look beyond ourselves and find creative, beneficial solutions. This is no easy task …. but that is why we need optimism."

Matthew Jones, Director, Oldowan

"My optimism is one of my most powerful assets – it brings an extraordinary advantage but also a responsibility to share and develop amongst others – customers, suppliers, partners, employees, peers and the broader industries I am privileged to serve.

"It's also important to consider the global context too. We live in a wonderful age – people are living longer, healthier and happier lives, Technology is radically changing the world, and our evolution. The global community is closer, more accessible and able to communicate across many real-time platforms. Sure this brings challenges and tension, but also development, opportunity and growth.

"How can you not be optimistic in all of this?"

Catherine Barrett, Director of Celebrate Ageing.

"I make a conscious decision every day to be optimistic – I acknowledge the difficulties and challenges and then choose to focus on what there is hope for. It brings joy into my life every day and has enabled me to be more resilient."

Jorden Lam, General Counsel, Hesta

"The privilege I have to make my own choices and the freedom that comes with that choice makes me optimistic about the future and its opportunities."

David Downs, Author of "A Mild Touch of the Cancer"

"I believe you can be an optimist or a pessimist, and whichever one you choose to practise, you'll probably get really good at it. I choose to be an optimist, and I practise it every day. And - more often than not - things turn out better."

Onisha Patel, structural biologist and artist at Walter and Eliza Hall Institute of Medical Research and a Superstar of STEM with Science & Technology Australia

"For me, optimism begins with trying something new and see where it takes you. Regardless of the outcome, it gives you a purpose and a sense of empowerment. Along the way, it is always good to look out for others and make them feel the same."

Sophie Davies, Australian Ambassador to Colombia & Venezuela

"My optimism comes from my belief in humanity, that most of us want to do good for each other, and the future is our destiny!"

Rik Schnabel

"Optimism is knowing that there is a grander purpose in everything."

Dr Sanam Mustafa, Molecular Pharmacologist and a 'Superstar of STEM'

"In research, 'failed' experiments, rejected manuscripts or unsuccessful funding applications can take their toll. I have learnt to deal with this by beginning each day with an optimistic outlook. Each day brings new opportunities, so start each day with the intention to find these. Dwelling on the past will only distract you!"

Cr Samantha McIntosh, Mayor of Ballarat

"Optimism gifts us the potential to make nothing something and something wonderful."

Voices of Optimistic Leadership

Dominic Barton, Global Managing Director, McKinsey

"Optimism is at the very core of leadership. The best leaders I have encountered in my career are those that remain optimistic -- and ambitious -- for their organisations even in the face of great adversity. They are those whose optimism enables them to recognise the potential in others, and help them develop to be leaders themselves."

President Bill Clinton

"I am the ultimate optimist: I always see the glass as half full"

Indonesian President Joko "Jokowi" Widodo

"A leader should convey optimism and encourage his or her people, even though there are many difficult challenges."

"There is no country on earth that prospers without optimism"

Scott Morrison, Prime Minister of Australia

"At the best of times and the worst of times I'm always optimistic."

President Tsai Ing-wen, Republic of China on Taiwan

"We will face the future with optimism and overcome challenges with determination."

Peter Pellegrini, Prime Minister of Slovakia

"I'm a very optimistic person"

Denis Henry, Chairman of the Royal Flying Doctor Service

"Optimism about the future and about the essential goodness in the majority of your community and workforce is the fuel for the certainty and commitment a leader needs."

Dr Tommy Weir

"A leader's optimism spreads further than their circle of support and radiates longer than the ring of the words. The optimistic leader describes what can be achieved. They talk about it. They're excited about it. They inspire others to see coming success. And more so, they give their teams a reason to embrace this belief."

Rebecca Elvy, Leading from Within

"Leadership is optimism in action. You cannot be a leader unless you believe that things can and will be better - and more importantly, better because of the intervention and action that you enable and empower. People might not see the way forward themselves, but you shine the light and show them the way. This must not be confused with a lack of realism, though. Because if you mislead people with blind optimism, you will lose their trust, and they will never again believe that the light they can see way off in the distance is actually the end of the tunnel."

Ron Wilson, CEO of Navy Health

"Every year in the last century, the world has got richer, healthier and more tolerant. Along the way, there have been many setbacks and too much suffering but we seem to retrieve the situation - leaders such as Churchill and Roosevelt defeated evil and Reagan, Thatcher and John Paul 11 defeated communism. Great leaders see to it that good overcomes evil."

Robert Masters, Chair, Centre for Optimism

"Leadership and optimism are the two key elements the community wants in today's unsettled world. Leaders must have optimism as the foundation for all their policies; and they must deliver it through sound, confident and stable leadership. Growth, employment, equality, innovation, tax, health, education, security all require this thinking. Communities not only expect it, but also deserve it."

Alma Besserdin, Wimmigrants Founder

"Optimism has been a key to humans helping them develop, progress and learn. Optimism and empathy is what we are looking for in our leaders."

Guy Kawasaki

"Optimism is a cornerstone of knowing how to lead a team. Learn how being optimistic can help leaders show their teams that the future looks bright."

Mark Moses

People are naturally drawn to leaders who see the world through a lens of optimism.

Ernie Bower, Founder of BowerGroupAsia

"Leadership requires optimism and the world requires optimistic leaders."

Melinda Muth, Management Educator and Company Director

"Positive leadership, the words and actions of the leader, sets the tone from the top. It leads to beneficial relationships which are at the heart of good decision-making and top performance. Positive leadership creates a virtuous cycle of beneficial relationships leading to effective conversations, and encouraging and affirmative language built on the power of positive words."

The Honourable Chris Pearce, MD of Lawson Delaney

"Optimism is an essential element in achievement and fulfillment not just at a personal level but also at an organisational level. Optimism is an infectious factor in assisting people to become leaders and to make changes in their day-to-day lives."

Charles Figley, Tulane University

"Leaders who are optimistic have the ability to see the 'opportunities' in adversity and believe in a positive outcome."

Diane G. Tillman, Living Values Author

"Optimistic leadership is very needed at this critical juncture in the world. While some governments and many NGOs are moving toward positive solutions to the environmental and the plethora of social challenges, other governments and radical groups are engaged in blatant injustice and violence. Optimistic leadership generates hope; it nourishes the belief that all will be well. This belief is important for emotional wellbeing; it fuels greater cooperation and harmony in the community and workplace with tangible benefits in productivity, health and happiness. But optimistic leadership must be paired with values to be sustainable. Optimistic leadership paired with guile and egocentric selfishness deceives over time, generating mistrust, cynicism, and hopelessness, fear or hate. Optimistic leadership paired with respect for others empowers. I feel we need leaders who deeply understand the importance of inclusion and equality. A visible commitment to the values of peace, respect and equality help ameliorate the feelings of exclusion and bitterness which fuel violence and unite us to work for the common good. Optimistic leadership based on respect for all creates hope, positive solutions, a sense of belonging, and humanizes us all."

Professor Sandra Levitsky, University of Michigan

"I believe there is tremendous power in optimism. And I'm not talking about emotional power or psychological power. I'm actually talking about real political power."

Fiona Lang, COO, BBC Worldwide Aust & NZ

"As an optimist, I love that leadership inspiration exists all around us if we are prepared to look for it. You can see it watching on the side line of school or club sport. You can see it in the more tender and heartfelt moments watching as friends or colleagues go through tough times when they keep moving forward. What they are really doing is leading themselves through change. And, you can see it every day in business, in the behaviours and values we expect from each other. What we accept or do not accept defines our leadership."

Shannon Togawa Mercer

"Optimism is political power."

Rod Sims, Chair, ACCC

"The more optimistic you are the more you will achieve. Pessimism means you achieve less as it is very hard to exceed your own expectations."

Dr Louise Schaper

"To lead with meaning and to live with meaning, you must dare to be optimistic."

Justin Johnson

"I am absolutely optimistic about the future. It is what we make it! Leadership is all about having a vision, sharing it with others and bringing them along. There seems to be a lot of disruptive forces and threats in the world today - but there has always been disruption and there will always be threats. We as a people have more knowledge and capacity that at any time in our history - could we screw it up? Of course! But I am confident we won't, that good leaders will cut through the noise and lead us to a bright future. It won't be linear, there will be miss-steps and side trips - but that is the way it has always been."

John Pesutto

"I'm optimistic because we get so little time to do good. Because of all the pressures, all the challenges that confront leadership, you have to make the most of every opportunity you have. You can't afford, in my view, to dwell or obsess about all the things that can go wrong or that are in your way. There is a joy, a real joy, in achieving something, particularly as a political leader, on behalf of the people you represent. And it might be something little or something unexpected, or it might be something even grander. "

Theresa Moltoni OAM, President of the Chamber of Commerce & Industry Queensland

"Optimism in leadership destroys the barriers to success. Embracing optimism empowers us to ignore the obstacles that might otherwise prevent us from reaching our potential as organisations, as communities, as teams, as families and as individuals."

Yasmahne Hanel, Director Industry Development & Policy, Queensland Department of Tourism

Optimism can't exist without leadership - it is required to inspire, grow and develop. People won't follow if there is no dream or aspiration to stretch for.

Gillian Fox

"Optimism isn't fostered by accident. Leaders are conscious about being optimistic and energetic in their role."

Ann Fastiggi and Darleen DeRosa

"Optimists make strong leaders since they are open to innovation, demonstrate big picture thinking, inspire employees and deal with adversity with a positive attitude"

Kay Clancy, Transformation Specialist

"Optimism is not just a "doing", at its core I believe that optimism is a "being". Like a candle lights the path and provides hope and a way of seeing in the darkness, so optimism offers an anchor that the power to improve what is happening is ours and that joy can guide our outlook. It's easy to get caught up in the busyness of "doing". I often ask myself "Who am I being that is contributing to the reality I see around me?" Leaders who focus on their "being" with as much energy and enthusiasm as their "doing" will set an infectious stream of optimism running far and wide with an impact that is beyond measure."

Frank Smallwood, Barcaldine Regional Council

"In my opinion, optimism is driven from the top. If our business leaders are optimistic about the future, their actions will likely lead to more opportunity. If there is sustained optimism, this could and should filter down to create opportunities at the very base level. I believe our current optimism is likely to go that deep."

Robert Hillard, Managing Partner, Deloitte Consulting

"There is a tendency to make the case for change based on the downside, whether it be trade, manufacturing, STEM capability, energy or the environment it is often easier to describe a dystopian future and challenge the status quo. In fact, when we look at the rate of change in Australia across almost every dimension it is greater than at any time in the working lives of anyone in business or government today. What's more, many of the structural inefficiencies that held us back are gradually fading away. Business and government are partnering across industries and the federal/state divide in ways that were almost impossible just a few years ago: Transport infrastructure is being built; Advanced manufacturing is taking hold; and, New energy technologies have, arguably, gained critical mass. No one leader can take credit and it would be tempting to imagine what would be possible if there were such a person. Having said that, many individuals are playing their part across many sectors."

Dr Steve Weitzenkorn, Co-author, The Catalyst Effect

Great leaders, regardless of their role or title, invigorate with optimism to achieve extraordinary results. Optimistic leadership has the power to galvanize — to catalyze — and be a force for driving an organization to new heights, turning performance around, and rebuilding momentum.

Extensive research has shown that optimism generates purposeful energy, creative thinking, and a drive for results. It propels and creates a belief in great possibilities. Intel cofounder Robert Noyce said optimism is "an essential ingredient of innovation. How else can the individual welcome change over security, adventure over staying in safe places?" Invigorating with Optimism, one of the 12 competencies described in *The Catalyst Effect*, conveys a can-do spirit. Can't-do advocates are quick to cite reasons why something cannot be accomplished and why efforts to try are a waste of time and energy. If naysayers had prevailed, people would have never landed on the moon; laparoscopic surgery that reduces body trauma, pain, scarring, and recovery time would not have been developed; and you wouldn't have a smartphone in your pocket or bag. All of these, and far more, came about because optimists believed they were possible — which triggered high-energy, catalytic undertakings that brought them to fruition.

Central to Invigorating with Optimism is the strong and shared belief that a team or organization can rise to great heights, whether from great depths or the middle of the pack, and excel with its own winning formula.

Peter Crawley, MD of Growing Innovations Management

"Optimism is inbred in us all that is how we got this far over the past millennia. It is the seed from the dream planted in those that follow (tribe, clan, families, workers, defenders and the young) by the leaders that stand up raise the flag and gain consensus to plan the pathways they will confidently as one stride. The highway lit bright by optimism, trust, loyalty and the belief that action is the guide and direction toward attainment, achievement fulfillment. The case for optimism... is in the proof from where we have come and knowing there are many many millennia still to travel, together!"

Wade Kapszukiewicz, Mayor, City of Toledo, Ohio

"I'm not sure if I have the "Character of the Happy Warrior" that William Wordsworth wrote about so many years ago. I just know it's easier to lead people when you do so with a smile on your face and a twinkle in your eye."

Fi Bendall, Chief Executive Officer at Bendalls Group

"In an era where people's mistrust of government and business is at all-time high. Where we as people simply don't believe and at times don't believe in each other, optimism needs to thrive. But how? Humans need hope and hope needs humans. The most amazing stories of human kindness, and warmth still permeate this "mistrusting world" we live in. In a world crisis, everyday heroes rise to the top in their kindness to others. In terror on our streets, people rush to help people. On the street look around you for daily inspiration to be optimistic…only today I saw people on the street rushing to help an old lady with her groceries that had spilt all over the sidewalk in Manhattan. The human being still embodies hope and optimism to drive and change our world for better. The more technology speeds at us, the more we need to touch and feel human kindness. Kindness breeds optimism, and optimism breeds hope. We have to hold on to that as our pessimism and mistrust is a weakness, our optimism and belief is our true power and empowerment."

Nina Greig-Towers, The Future Business Council

"Not being optimistic about your work, your team or about you illustrates that something major is failing or there are deep failures in your work. Whatever it may be to be a leader is to give hope, happiness, education, motivation and so on. Not being optimistic doesn't allow you to believe in the impossible, thus your team never striving for the impossible."

Doug Kimberley, Pumpa Manufacturing

"The Case for Optimism? At last I see most employer representatives organisations recognizing the need to focus on leadership not just management. There is express focus on risk taking as well as risk management and there is a drive to recognise the need for and reality of innovation at the day to day level. Innovative thinking allows more innovation at all organization levels."

Donna Petrovich, Former Member of Parliament

"With such a sceptical community, trust and integrity in leadership are vital in re building faith in leadership. We need charismatic and credible leaders who deliver outcomes! I am optimistic."

Neil Kuruppu, CEO of PepperStack Global

"I believe that optimism is a by-product of leadership. Leadership is the sincerely crazy belief that one can shape the world. I sometimes feel that I am walking a tight-rope that is tethered at one end and where people see a haze in front, I see the rope is definitely tethered at the other and I am convincing people to follow me on that tight-rope. Those who do follow believe in my belief. Call it optimism if you like, but in my opinion it is unbridled self-conviction that a leader can truly change the world for the better despite all the impeding forces around us. In conclusion focusing on the 'noise of negativity' is not an option if you are walking a tight rope."

Derek Rowe, Creator of CSAR

"Keep the word leadership and remove optimism and what are you left with? Hopelessness. Hope is the epicentre of leadership, framing EI, trust, consultation and all the other traits that usually appear in those top 10 lists of what leaders need. Hope. Without it, why lead? Where are you headed? Mandela, Churchill, Jobs, Gandhi. They all had hope, at times against all odds. It's where belief in self, others, causes, products etc. comes from. Optimism and hope? Pretty much the same thing I reckon."

Evelyn Moolenburgh, Leadership Expert

"Optimism is paramount. I think you just have to go for it if you have a business idea. There is so much support around these days whether it's incubators or the internet which are full of advice or you can read books or get mentors. There's every opportunity to start your own business and I think if you're optimistic about the future and set good plans then you have every chance of being successful."

David Dowsey,

"The world needs and is primed for optimistic leaders. They are the ones that start the fire, inspire others to follow them, dig deep within themselves and extract the best in those around them. They are the ones with the big dreams and the capacity to make them happen. But they often need help from other 'types' in order to fully complete their mission. In their enthusiasm for making a difference and getting things done they sometimes fail to recognise this. It is vital that an optimistic leader has an 'observer' close to them on their team and that they use that person as a trusted sounding board. That person is the typical INTP on the Myers Briggs Type Indicator and they have the capability to challenge and 'check' any 'over-reaching' or unrealistic beliefs or desires on behalf of the optimistic leader. The 'observer' by nature is often quiet, perhaps aloof. That's because they are noticing what is happening around them and evaluating risk and reward. They can sometimes appear negative and may sometimes frustrate the optimistic leader, but the optimistic leader needs them. This is the Yin and Yang of life; the way things should be. The 'observer' often makes good decisions and are there for the optimistic leader when they 'jump' too readily. If the optimistic leader wanted to go skydiving, it would be the 'observer' that they would want with them to check their parachute."

Ron Jones

"There is hope. My own view of leadership is that what separates leaders from managers is the focus on 'purpose': defining purpose for ourselves, for our organisations and for our community is the essence of what shapes the future. No-one leads for the past - they lead for the future. So the very nature of leadership is that it is something we can all contribute to according to our purpose. When each of us is asked to express our purpose it seems to me that this cannot be done without being optimistic. Even where the circumstances or events that we face are in themselves tragic, there is an emergence of ourselves as better able to learn from the experience to shape a better future."

Elizabeth Vega, CEO of Informed Solutions

"It often said that people who are depressed tend to be fixated on a past that they can't change or go back to. People who are anxious, tend to worry about a future that they can't control. The most balanced and optimistic people are generally those that make the most of the opportunities in the here and now. Just saying, however, I suspect that they also make the best leaders and role models.'

Liz Conway

"I would like to see leadership as people who 'will stand for something rather than fall for anything.' Leaders who aren't afraid to stand for what is right and true regardless of the consequences (thinking of politics here). Or without regard to the polls! Leaders who inspire confidence and who inspire others to lead."

Alex de Waal, CEO at Greyhound Australia

Both optimistic & pessimistic mindsets have the propensity to prevail, one leads to discovery & the other to desperation. I have yet to discover a positive solution born from a desperate mind, whereas desperate situations often bear extraordinary solutions!

Professor Paul Gadek

"Leaders have a vision for the future and a conviction that it is achievable and will be good for those they lead. Optimism to me implies a hope rather than a pathway. But I do hope for the best, whatever that turns out to be."

Cheryl Lacey, Learning and Development Consultant

"Integrity is life's mirror. For those in leadership it's what matters most. When you share your greatest lessons with honesty, and with a strong moral compass to guide you, you are closer to being whole and undivided. Ultimately, despite what anyone else thinks of you, integrity is about what you think of yourself. And with integrity comes optimism."

Warren Bennis, Leadership Expert

"Every exemplary leader that I have met has what seems to be an unwarranted degree of optimism – and that helps generate the energy and commitment necessary to achieve results."

Kristen Hansen

"According to a study of 5400 executives by Macquarie University, Australian National University and the University of NSW, people in high-performance workplaces feel more valued, proud, optimistic, cheerful and loved than those in low-performing workplaces."

Time's Nancy Gibbs asked Bill Gates which world leaders today make him optimistic?

"There are some amazing leaders, like Chancellor Angela Merkel in Germany. She got a lot of criticism for bringing in refugees. She's been a great leader in terms of thinking about the world and having a good, calm view of things. Leadership in India has been quite good. There's a lot of things about reforming the country and getting it to be a bit less socialistic and trying to get things moving, so they tap their potential. There's no Nelson Mandela, where there's somebody who took a country and did something where we completely wouldn't have expected that to take place. Indonesia has good leadership. In a lot of the African countries that traditionally had sort of tribal thinking, which doesn't run the country well, there's been a slight increase in the number of democracies."

Christine Lagarde, Head of the European Bank

"I'm optimistic. It's my nature."

Shiekh Mohammed, PM, United Arab Emirates

"I am optimistic about the future. I always look as the glass as half full. As much as the "Arab Fall" was costly, its lessons were valuable. I believe that the majority of the leaderships in the Arab world have learned these lessons"

Bruna Martinuzzi

"Optimism is a key leadership trait for anyone leading teams. It can be especially important for anyone who leads an entrepreneurial venture where risk and uncertainty are common, and where an optimistic outlook for the future can help stay the course. But being optimistic doesn't mean being bullheaded and refusing to face facts. And it doesn't mean going around wearing the proverbial rose-colored glasses. It's about being inclined to hope. It's leading teams by showing them that you have confidence in a better tomorrow no matter what false starts or setbacks the team may be facing today."

Elissa Newall, CEO of the Plato Project

"Leaders must have optimism. How else can you imagine a better future and inspire others to join you working to achieve it?"

Dale Crownover, CEO, Texas NamePlate

"I'm excited. I'm more optimistic. Leaders have got to have a sense of optimism. I'm already am an optimistic type person. It's given me a lot of incentives. It gives me a lot more drive."

Joel Garfinkle

"The art of being truly optimistic lies not only in the ability to keep a positive attitude in adverse situations, but also in being able to offer sincere, realistic leadership that gets the team through the hardship in one piece. No one is looking to have sunny platitudes hashed out or unrealistic predictions made. Great leaders can be positive in the face of difficulty and still be very much in touch with the situation."

Will Hodgman, Premier of Tasmania

"My father taught me; live every day like it's your last. If you do that, every day you'll focus on the future, what you can do to make a positive impact, and be thankful when you can do it all again tomorrow."

David Cameron, Former PM of the United Kingdom

"Dad's gift to me was his optimism... My dad, who was disabled, taught me about optimism – that no matter how bad things are, you can overcome them if you have the right frame of mind. Indeed, if there's one gift my father gave me that I cannot thank him enough for, it was his ability to always look on the bright side of life."

Charles Fairlie, Publisher and Writer

“I’ve interviewed 75 business leaders and met with many more. As you’d expect, in all cases they were optimistic people by nature, that goes without saying. But it’s their ability to inspire others through communication of that optimism, whether via story-telling or other indirect mechanisms, to motivate and mobilise other people into action”

George T. Cummings

“Leadership is the ability to see what no one else sees, to listen when others talk and the ability to be optimistic when others are pessimistic.”

Steve Gutzler

"People want to follow leaders who are upbeat, optimistic, and confident about the future!"

Jeremy Johnson, President , Australian Chamber

Optimism is an essential ingredient of effective leadership. Its infectiousness inspires commitment to the cause. It makes people feel good about participating in the mission at hand and embracing the challenges of the tasks that need to be accomplished for ultimate success.

Lucia Cade, Chair of South East Water

"I think optimism is an essential ingredient to being an action and solution-oriented decision maker.

I find that the more I listen to others with an open mind a genuine curiosity about their point of view and ideas, the more great solutions emerge that are better than the sum of the parts. And the broader I cast that net, the more interesting the ideas and the better the solutions.

I also believe that opportunity and optimism create the environment for achievement which builds into a virtuous cycle of success. I have observed that in providing people with the opportunity to be a part of positive change, to have a personal impact on creating a better service, a better community outcome, a better business, whatever area of endeavour, that they rise to the challenge.

I am not optimistic all the time but fortunately, it is the state I swing back to as my equilibrium."

Uschi Schreiber

"Optimism is inherent to good leadership - it's all about creating a vision for a better future and instilling that optimistic view in others."

Michelle Marks PhD, Founder of Psychological Fitness Training™

"I view optimism more as an attitude than an attribute, and one that's essential to have in the tool-box of effective leaders. By strategically using optimistic thinking to reframe negative events as learning opportunities rather than catastrophes, and to view setbacks as temporary challenges rather than permanent obstacles, we can remain focused on our most meaningful goals. And by consciously deciding to choose hope over doubt, we can navigate the sometimes-choppy waters of our lives with confidence and enthusiasm. As a practical person, and not an optimist by nature, I've learned that there's a time for optimism, and that's most of the time, but some situations benefit from a more objective lens. The ability to choose when to use that lens exemplifies the mental agility of the most psychologically fit among us – those with the potential to be dynamic and masterful leaders."

Repa Patel, Executive Coach and Yoga Teacher

"When a leader engages the hearts and minds of their team by articulating the deeper impact of their work, it connects to a higher purpose and provides meaning and optimism beyond economic transactions."

Korn Ferry

"Optimism is the degree to which people tend to disregard disappointment, are satisfied with who they are, and expect the future to be bright. Successful leadership requires a steady healthy optimism and good expectations for the future."

Anthony Gruppo

"The recognition of success must always be greater than the discussion of failure. Optimism is the insulation to protect a leader from the negativity of doubt."

Jim Spigener

"Leadership does not exist without optimism. Optimism is the secret to motivation, happiness and self-worth!"

Lisa Jasper

"Being an optimistic leader is not about rainbows and roses, blind optimism or going wherever the wind blows and believing that everything will work itself out. Instead, it's an intelligent approach to reframing how you think about business."

Chris Reddy, Leadership Coach

"The best leaders aren't those who speak the loudest or are most decisive. The best leaders I have seen are those who share their vision, inspire self-belief, listen and learn from this around them. To infect optimism on those around me, I challenge negative thinking, promote positive relationships and look to celebrate and praise the small things as well as the big."

Jeff Rigby, Managing Director, Coliban Water

"Leaders do what needs to be done when it needs to be done. Optimistic leaders have the self-belief and conviction that they can do it"

Jo Mikleus

"Optimism in leadership embodies essential qualities required to lead in a fast-paced and ever-changing world. I think the valuable qualities of an optimistic leader include self-awareness, flexibility, self-confidence, initiative, resilience, and adaptability. Having an optimistic outlook creates conditions for success as it allows leaders to recognise and redirect unhelpful reactions, to think before acting, and to choose positive responses. Leaders who are optimistic generally raise the aspirations of their teams to aspire towards (and achieve) their best. They do this by creating an environment that blends vision with personal accountability, innovative thinking and appropriate risk-taking."

Kirsten Lloyd

"The definition of optimism in leadership resides quite simply in the dogged determination to believe in tomorrow"

Mark Williamson, CEO of Action for Happiness

"Authentic leaders are realists as well as optimists, able to show vulnerability, admit mistakes and to compromise where necessary for the greater good."

Nina Anderson, Founder of Anderson Advisory

"I am a natural optimist so I look for upside in everything - even drought and pestilence!

"I think it's really important for leaders to be able to stand back from a situation, even when the chips are down, to reflect and to see the upside, the opportunities and the lessons you can learn.

"I constantly ask myself, why am I doing this, what's good about it and what am I learning. It's important to be realistic, but if you focus on the negatives you get bogged down and progress becomes a struggle."

Sandra Gates, Director of Allied Health and Clinical Support Services, The Royal Women's Hospital.

"Optimism is essential to enable us to reach our potential and be truly effective leaders."

Paul Eleftheriou, Chief Medical Officer, Western Health
"A half-full glass is what we must always perceive, but in leadership, we must also seek out a larger glass, that perpetually needs filling"

Jimmy Wales, Founder of Wikipedia

"I'm a pathological optimist."

Simon Bridges New Zealand's Leader of the Opposition

1. "We are not defined by our circumstances and get out of life what we put in. Every day is a chance to do good while enjoying this life to the max."
2. "I am unapologetically optimistic about what New Zealanders can continue to achieve on the world stage, and what the Government can do to represent our interests."

Mary-Lou O'Brien, Chief Digital Officer at Melbourne Girls Grammar.

"For me optimism is a mindset. A choice each of us makes. We all have options and I choose to be an optimist, even in the most negative situations. It's just a matter of focusing on the potential upside and whilst sometimes it takes time and patience, there is always an upside. An optimistic outlook imbues options for others, making it a valuable trait for leaders at all levels"

Babette Bensoussan

"I have had the privilege and honour to work with a number of outstanding CEOs who have courage, integrity, honesty and are willing to explore themselves to lead in better ways... What is there not to be optimistic about?"

Pauline McKinnon, Founding Director, Stillness Meditation Therapy Centre

Optimists have a can-do attitude built into their belief system that enables them to persevere through to achievement, despite challenge. Many optimists would claim the benefit of spiritual faith which in turn offers the strength of hope in the face of adversity. The optimist also knows the importance of remaining calm and trusting oneself to find – or wait for – the solution.

A leader conceives ideas, trusts them, believes in them, practices them and follows then through. A leader has the confidence to draw the support of others - and remains optimistic despite discouragement or disappointment, finding new ways to express his or her passion.

Angela Kambouris

"Optimism is the essence of every conscious leader: The belief that no matter what you will find a way. Optimism is a precursor to success and the optimistic leader encourages a culture of creative thinking.

Karen Grima, Coordinator of Economic Development at Brimbank City Council.

"I love the quote 'nothing great was ever achieved without enthusiasm' and I'm more than a little Pollyanna in my approach in personal and work life - always looking for the positives in any/every situation. I have two girls who I've told since they were little to always look for the positives, even in the worst situation the positives are usually there, they'll just need digging out.

I think optimism and being an optimistic leader (or being led by one) makes for a braver workplace and creates a willingness to try out new ideas."

Sonia McDonald, Leadership Author and Speaker

"Optimistic leadership is about being brave, kind and courageous as a leader. To be optimistic means knowing that we can overcome anything. The power of being focused on being true and kind to oneself and others is leadership."

Jack Berckemeyer and Debbie Silver

"Principals Should Be the School Optimist-in-Chief."

Nicholas Abbey, co-creator of The Great Schools Network

Optimistic leaders help to generate persistence and grit in a strategic course of action and real change that is challenging and difficult.

By being truly strategic and progressive, these leaders may show that optimism is not a blind or naïve positivity, but is about people's collaborative power and shared leadership and decision-making in going further and faster together to achieve significant breakthroughs in outcomes.

In short, true optimism is aligned with shared leadership guiding great, practical strategies in order to achieve great things together.

Dr Kathy Nicholson, COO, ARC Centre of Excellence for Nanoscale BioPhotonics

"Optimistic leaders believe that today's small victories will lead us towards a better tomorrow."

Alf Dunbar, Creator and Director of You Are The Difference.

"People want to follow leaders who are upbeat, optimistic, have a solid plan and are confident about the future."

Janet Dore

"Leadership is classically a two-way street between the "boss" and the "workers" which entails mutual beliefs based on trust. Such trust is built on the observed behaviours of all leaders in the business. So optimistic leadership better be founded on facts and supported with tools for the job or the B.S. meter will sound the alarm. No room for complacency either way but it's exhilarating when it works."

Natalie Scanlon, Founding Director of Written Communications

"When considering the impact of optimism on leadership I ask myself the following: Can an influential and innovative leader afford to forego optimism? If yes, what are the consequences of actively disregarding any form of positive thinking when considering initial policy making, or even initiation of modern-day legislation? In my opinion, the answer is a resounding no. Optimism cannot be carelessly disregarded. This is because optimism is an imperative and necessary component of development. It initiates change, and encourages risk so that the impossible can be achieved. Optimism encourages personal growth, an empathetic understanding of others and is, realistically, the key difference between mediocre and phenomenal."

David Bartlett, Former Premier of Tasmania

"I think leadership and optimism are deeply entwined and related. Optimists see what can be and get more done. I am deeply optimistic about the next generation of leaders because they are largely blind to colour, religion, gender and sexuality. They don't see those things... they see talent, opportunity and solutions."

Karen Gately

"With the right environment created by great leaders with courage, integrity and infectious optimism, human beings will find the solutions to our problems whether they be in business or on a global scale. We have the intelligence: I am optimistic."

Margie Stewart, C2 Melbourne

"Optimism is essential for all leaders. It enables them to share a positive vision and inspire their teams. They are able to empower and encourage individuals to take a risk and leap of faith. Optimistic leaders are creative and able to find solutions to problems. They don't get stuck fixating on spreadsheets and tiny details. They keep sight of the big picture and what is really important. Their focus is always on their customers, internal and external stakeholders. Their optimism creates a culture that is inclusive and brings out the best in people. They are forward thinking and always moving towards success and positive outcomes for all."

Andrew Baylis, Leadership expert

"It is said that luck is really just where opportunity is recognised and action ensues. I'd argue that to be optimistic we only need the following:

Have a dream;

Have the tools / power / opportunity to act upon your dream;

Be able to act yourself (i.e. not be waiting for someone else to do it all);

Recognise when the opportunity exists and have the courage to try something.

If you look through this list, it is pretty easy to be optimistic and Australia is a great country in which this can happen. The biggest challenge is the fourth point and this is where some can come unstuck..."

David Worland, Chief Executive Officer, Australian Childcare Alliance Victoria

"The ability to identify and action the need for change positively is an integral component of leadership. Facing difficult situations positively is not always easy and often requires great courage. Of course, appropriate risk management will accompany change management."

Leonie Walsh, Chair, Centre for New Energy Technologies

"Optimistic leaders understand the challenges at hand but choose to focus on the opportunities and solutions. They get the best for and from their team and share in the success. I am fortunate to know a number of leaders that have inspired this belief."

Melanie Gentgall, CEO of Praxis Australia

"It's OK to show your vulnerability at times and show how through optimism you can bounce back from the lows to reach the next high."

Rebekah Foster, Central Highlands Water

"An optimistic leader welcomes change over security and adventure over staying in safe places. They may not be the lead decision-maker in an organisation but rather the one with the ability to bring people on the journey to challenge the norm and welcome the unknown."

Chris Webb, Head of Regulatory, EPA Victoria.

"I am optimistic because I choose to be. Natural or unconscious optimism is a great team and leadership trait, but being able to consciously choose to switch it on can be really powerful. Optimism allows you to see the positive possibilities before the barriers. Using it consciously helps you find pathways through complex issues and opening up new approaches to old problems."

Voices of Contagious Optimism

I believe the best leaders are contagious (infectious) optimists and lead their teams to discover greater optimism, resilience and self-mastery. These thoughts from Bertrand and others sing to me.

Bertrand Badré, World Economic Forum's Co-Chair Global Future Council

"Leadership must appropriately combine a harsh sense of reality with a dose of contagious optimism. It is about looking forward past the obstacles. Yes we can!"

Malka Lawrence, Chair, TMG College

"Optimism is contagious, if you believe it can happen you inspire others to also believe and as a group working collaboratively, each with their strengths and expertise, everything is possible"

Chris Webb, Head of Regulatory, EPA Victoria.

"I work around lots of optimistic people - what is it that makes this group stand out? I saw in another of your posts the word "contagious", and I think that's the difference. To me, the word infectious creates a picture of the optimism that rubs off on everyone in the room. The word contagious I think captures the effect where everyone leaves the room and carries it with them. That is how I would characterise those I've included in my list - their optimistic leadership that impacts beyond the moment and shapes the way the team functions."

Mimi Kwa, Presenter and MC

"Optimism and kindness are contagious. They are good for the heart and soul. They improve heart function, overall health and well-being and they cost you nothing. Your reasons for spreading positivity and kindness are unimportant. Do it selfishly to help your physical and mental health. Or do it selflessly and altruistically. The result is the same. So just do it."

Deborah Sweeney, CEO of MyCorporation.com

"The beauty of a positive attitude is that it is contagious. When you are optimistic and see the glass as half-full, others around you will catch on to that feeling. Be the most energetic you that you can be. Get a good night's sleep, eat healthy, and make time to exercise and read so you are able to nurture the self-care side of yourself. Share all of your ideas, and your great attitude, with your team, colleagues, partners, and vendors. People want to be around positive individuals. They'll stick around for a positive entrepreneur, and work with them no matter what. Be that to others and watch as your connections and opportunities grow!"

Jon Gordon, President, Jon Gordon Companies

"Lead with Optimism (it's contagious!) - The engine for America's growth and prosperity has always been its can-do attitude and spirit. Unfortunately, in the past few years optimism has been in short supply. The most important weapon against pessimism is to transfer your optimism and vision to others. Leadership is a transfer of believe and your belief inspires others to think and act in ways that drive results."

Kare Anderson, Author and Speaker

"Now, more than ever, we need to step out of our filter bubbles and befriend others with diverse views and complementary talents so we can see more sides to situations, make smarter decisions, be able to recruit apt people to seize opportunities and solve problems faster and better. My case for optimism is that those who adopt a mutuality mindset and see healthy relationships as not a quid pro quo yet an ebb and flow of mutual support over time, as Give and Take author, Adam Grant advises, will generate experiences that can make them feel optimistic about their "greater good" impact. This is especially needed in this tech enabled era where The Law of Unintended Consequences is increasingly becoming the norm, not the exception. Since some research shows that negative behavior is more contagious than positive, it behooves us to advocate and collectively support specific methods and systems and companies and political leaders who adopt that constructive, mutuality mindset. And getting specific boosts self-clarity, credibility and memorability -- and reduces the chance that others will misunderstand you. Opportunity Makers, with and for others, tend to be optimistic because they see positive results of their actions."

****

Voices for Optimism and Action

Gary W. Moore, Author of 'Playing with the Enemy'

"Remain hopeful. Be optimistic. Believe in your dreams and act, not stopping until victory is at hand."

Tim Diamond , General Manager, The Cotton On Foundation

"Optimism is a way of life; it not only helps determine & create your own pathway but it projects its qualities to others around you. I owe my success and learnings through failure to optimism - and the work we do, is driven by an eternal optimism, one that hopes and expects that the world can be a better place. Always. That optimism demands action and drives an ever-better mentality."

Rosanna Iacono, Co-Founder, The Growth Activists

"Optimism is what fuels our hope, our resilience, our ability to pick ourselves and forge on in the face of failure, and most importantly our ability to create an exciting future vision to strive towards. But optimism is not fully potentialised until it is combined with thoughtful collective activism - only then are great things achieved."

The Honourable Jonathan O'Dea, Speaker of the NSW Parliament

"An attitude of optimism should involve more than just wishful thinking and prompt positive action. It can recognise that current reality is not ideal, while anticipating better things to come. True optimism creates confidence to push for change and confront inevitable difficulties in that journey. Remaining optimistic in these uncertain times is not naïve; rather, it is a reasonable expression of expectation and faith in a world that contains many signs of hope for the future."

Glenn Buesnel-May, Leadership Expert

"In geo-strategic terms, staying optimistic about the future is getting tough. I think the answer to pessimism is local, even private action. Putting your hands and heart into meaningful, social pursuits can give focus and a sense of purpose that enriches personal optimism and community capital. There's a tonne of studies that show how social pursuit and volunteering supports emotional health. No doubt a focus on helping and leading others can build optimism and enlighten any dark prognosis of the future."

Professor Maggie Cusack

"Optimism mobilises!"

Tanya Abreu

"Optimism is less attitude and more action. It is believing with every cell of your body that positive results are ALWAYS possible no matter what the circumstance."

Avi Liran

"Contributing is optimism in action. It translates hope into reality."

Jack Berckemeyer and Debbie Silver

Optimism is active. An optimistic leader isn't paralyzed by despair. Nor does the leader sit still and think positive thoughts. This leader learns everything possible about a situation, identifies options for response, makes a plan, and takes action.

Erik Solheim, Former Executive Director of the United Nations Environment Programme

"You cannot defeat hate with more hate, only with love.

"You cannot defeat hopelessness with pessimism, only with hope.

"We need the optimism of our will to inspire bold action!"

Francesc Badia i Dalmases

"Our duty is to be optimistic as a way to shape a better future for all."

Robert Cox, President of RCarlen Advisory Partners

"Being optimistic energizes me to Act, which often gets me involved in new and diverse Activities, which invariably turns me into We."

Alice Boer, Author

"Surely we should consider that optimism is also necessary for action. If you think everything's going to end up in the worst-case scenario, why bother doing anything? Yes, you need to harness your optimism and use it to spur you on to effect meaningful change, but the act of seeking change, and undertaking action is itself a fundamental act of optimism."

Voices for Optimism and Realism

Shannon Huffman Polson, Author

"We need more optimists, really. Realistic optimists. The only way anything gets done."

John Hagel, co-chairman for Deloitte LLP's Center for the Edge

"Optimism is the key to cultivating more of our human potential. We have infinite potential, but most of us tap into a very small portion of our potential because of fear or an inability to imagine the possibilities. Optimism is essential, but so is a realistic sense of the obstacles and roadblocks we will face on our journey. In fact, that is what will motivate us to make the journey because the opportunity is so big that it is worth addressing the challenges along the way."

Sheriff Russell L. Martin

"Inspirational & trustworthy leadership is always realistic but optimistic providing a message of hope & possibility"

Javier Fiz Pérez, Professor Psychology Università Europea di Roma

"A realist sees reality, and says, "This is real." An optimist sees his dreams, and says, "This will be real." An optimist will meet with greater success, will attain more of his dreams, is happier, grows more, and has better relationships and greater self-esteem than a pessimist. Perhaps in other times this would not have been the case, but in the society in which we are fortunate to live, where there are abundant opportunities, the environment favors optimists. Optimists will suffer more setbacks than realists, but actually, these difficulties are enriching experiences. In the not-very-remote past, or in other societies today, perhaps the most intelligent option would be to be a pessimistic realist and avoid disappointments. However, times have changed, and in places where opportunities abound, they favor the optimist."

Allen Little, School Principal

"Reality makes me optimistic. Because in reality, optimism is our natural state of being. We figure out how to be negative."

Professor John Hewson AM

"Perhaps the most disturbing aspect of recent politics has been its increasing negativity - the politics of NOPE rather than HOPE. A fundamental challenge of leadership is to provide realistic optimism, and to validate it by delivering against those expectations."

Professor Alan Duffy

"Scientists are the greatest optimists I know, how else could you confidently set out to uncover the secrets of our universe? But without a rigorous scientific method that optimism is just wishful thinking. Optimism and reason can solve any problem."

Mark Matthews, Chief Operations Officer at Business for Development, former soldier and diplomat

"Optimism is a source of inspiration, in ourselves as well as others. We want to connect with optimists! Optimism is not (just) bravery. It's the sense of creating positive, forward momentum. This does not give us the right to abrogate our responsibility and accountability for outcomes. We cannot be 'blind'. We have to have a strong sense of reality to navigate the path to success, as well as highly developed situational awareness - the foresight to predict and understand the consequences of our actions. Reflection and critique should not be seen as pessimism, nor an opportunity to cynically blame others for the things for which we are responsible."

Raya Bidshahri, Founder & CEO of Awecademy

"There is nothing to be gained from blind optimism. But an optimistic mindset can be grounded in rationality and evidence. It may be hard to believe, but we are living in the most exciting time in human history. Despite all of our ongoing global challenges, humanity has never been better off. Not only are we living healthier, happier, and safer lives than ever before, but new technological tools are also opening up a universe of opportunities."

Simon Terry

Optimism is tomorrow: Optimism is not inconsistent with realism because it does not describe today. Optimism is a hope for a better future. We can't be realistic about the future, only optimistic or pessimistic. All managers should embrace hope because it is the only way to validate their potential to be the actor that brings about improvement. If you don't have hope for your own influence, why are you there?

Kate Nasser

"Great leaders are optimistic and realistic. They have healthy scepticism without being pessimistic and jaded."

Sue Barrett, Author of the "Selling Better Manifesto"

"It all starts with opportunity. Opportunity makes it possible to do good things. Optimism is ignited when real opportunities for growth and prosperity become clear to us. Different from blind optimism, Purposeful Optimism is built on substance: derived from strategy and underpinned by well-resourced people who are enabled to pursue opportunity and do something meaningful with others. Optimism keeps the light of opportunity glowing even when the world seems dark."

Tim Kasser, Professor & Chair of Psychology, Knox College, Illinois and Author of *The High Price of Materialism*

"I've long told my students at Knox College that part of my job as their professor is to "pop their unrealistically optimistic bubbles." But I am not trying to make them into pessimists. Instead, I hope my students come to be realistic optimists, people who can look at whatever situation they face, assess it clearly and objectively, and then still believe that there is something they can do to improve their lives and the state of the world."

Sally Osberg, former CEO of the Skoll Foundation

“We’re incredibly optimistic about the potential for the world. At the same time, we’re driven by reality and the need to be rigorous, because the challenges are many and they’re morphing. It’s easy to feel overwhelmed sometimes, but that tough-minded optimism always served me and the foundation well.”

Dr Gary Small

"Healthy optimists are realistic — they can see the positive elements in their lives, but remain aware of their limitations. If we maintain a proper perspective on the positive aspects of our failures & negative experiences, we can cope better with anxiety"

Elena Carstoiu Hubgets COO & Co-founder

"I cover myself in many layers of realism, have a couple of pessimist facets, but deep down I strongly believe in humans. I’m an optimist touched by a healthy dose of reality check."

Ilona Jerabek

"Optimism isn't about pretending to be happy when you're not, acting like problems don't exist, or taking chances on blind faith. It also doesn't mean that you should repress your negative thoughts. Those are the kind of pie-in-the-sky optimists who refuse to accept reality as it is and can actually be quite reckless. The best outlook is optimism with a dose of realism. These are the optimists who recognize that there is a lesson in every negative situation and every failure. They prepare and plan ahead in case something could go wrong, but they also stay positive and focus on possibility, hope, and success. Most importantly, they understand that their outlook has a huge impact on their circumstances, and as our study and many other studies have shown, the benefits of being optimistic are numerous. You don't have to force yourself to be cheerful. Just strive to remember that how you view a situation impacts how you cope with it and how you approach it. So why not do so with an attitude of hope, promise, and positivity?"

Andrea Dempster-Chung

Realism and optimism can coexist: Optimists take a minute to process the facts and learn the lessons, but they also genuinely believe that a better opportunity could be just around the corner, so they tend to persevere"

Professor Joseph Lo Bianco, Professor of Language and Literacy Education at the Melbourne Graduate School of Education

"In general terms I would call myself a realist rather than an optimist. I know that things go wrong, that there is much injustice in the world, but that there are many reasons and benefits to be had from a more optimistic outlook, however I do not believe it can always be justified on the evidence around us. I have a clear and present pessimistic streak, which I believe would overwhelm if allowed to and so I must combat it. I usually confront the pessimism with a forced dose of realistic analysis and as a result I occasionally enjoy the fruits of the optimist's worldview. So, I cannot claim to be naturally either optimistic nor pessimistic, I am realistic about events and circumstances. I recognise that some people are disposed towards optimism, either for themselves or more generally for the social environment of which they are a part, and some are even optimistic about the world in the most general terms. Others are pessimistic in an identical mirror of the optimists. I think neither is entirely warranted, nor wrong. I also recognise that from a personal point of view an optimistic outlook is healthier, and provides more resilience in life. Optimism itself can become a resource for improvement, whereas pessimism can and does drag people down, infecting the individual with a defeatist attitude that itself causes failure, sadness and worse. In light of all this I believe the ideal would be to have personal optimism, leavened by a realistic appreciation of constraints, difficulties and injustices. I cannot assess whether I personally achieve this."

Voices for Optimism and Personal Growth

John Hagel, co-chairman for Deloitte LLP's Center for the Edge

"Optimism is the key to cultivating more of our human potential. We have infinite potential, but most of us tap into a very small portion of our potential because of fear or an inability to imagine the possibilities. Optimism is essential, but so is a realistic sense of the obstacles and roadblocks we will face on our journey. In fact, that is what will motivate us to make the journey because the opportunity is so big that it is worth addressing the challenges along the way."

Hon Philip Dalidakis, Australia Post

"Optimism is more than just a word or a noun, it's a way of defining our attitude to overcoming everyday adversity. Regardless of the challenges, good and bad, tomorrow always provides us with a new start, a new opportunity of improving on yesterday. And therein lies the ultimate understanding. Optimism isn't a destination, but one long continuous journey, in our personal & professional lives."

Melis Senova, Author of "This Human"

"It's better to think of positive future outcomes rather than negative ones. They are both equally likely because both are yet to happen! It feels better when you think about positive scenarios than negative ones, so you might as well."

Professor Erwin Loh, Chief Medical Officer, Monash Health

"Be an optimist, and be relentless in pursuing the beacon of hope, so that you are always moving towards the light that will guide you, shine on you, and keep the shadows of darkness and despair behind you. You will also make it easier for others to find you, follow you, and be inspired by you. And by moving together in the same positive direction of hope, instead of fear, you can change the world."

Bryna Kranzler, Author of "The Accidental Anarchist"

"It isn't the circumstances of our lives that determine who we are, but rather how we respond to them. Believing in a positive outcome -- even against all odds -- allows a solution for a seemingly intractable problem to present itself. And being aware of what is going right even when in dire circumstances makes it possible to recognize other positive events in your direction."

Roland Weber

"Optimism creates opportunities and allows you to rally people around you. SMART goals in both personal and business life and an open mind strongly aid in building a case for optimism which will foster growth both within and surrounds."

Emiliyan Gikovski

"We each have the power to set the tone for the things we do, the way we work, the relationships we have and foster, the personal interests we pursue and enjoy; this is directly linked to the level of optimism or, said another way, the level of positive and growth mindset that we adopt and practice in everything we do; the only limitations are those we set for ourselves."

Peter Kronborg, Chair, Wise Counsel Associates

"Consider Optimism as the top end of a simple straight bar magnet. It is an invisible energy that attracts good and feels good. And Pessimism is at the other end. It repels and feels bad. We can't always be at the optimistic end but if we generally flow and feel into that energy then Like will attract Like. Simple !"

Dr John Medina, Author of "Brain Rules"

"Optimism is not just emotional insulation against the freezing wastes of mortality. We now know that elders who have positive, even optimistic, attitudes toward their own aging live longer than those who don't. What do I mean by optimistic aging? A twenty-five-year-old who forgets somebody's name seldom considers it a harbinger of Alzheimer's disease. But if you're older and your memory transmission slips a gear, you might very well worry about Alzheimer's. You may become stressed, even depressed. As other roadside attractions of age come into view—from hearing loss to aching joints—your attitude may turn increasingly pessimistic. The data say: don't go there. Seniors who take it in stride, convincing themselves the glass is still half-full, live a healthy 7.5 years longer than seniors who don't. Optimism exerts a measurable effect on their brain. The volume of their hippocampus doesn't shrink nearly as much as the glass-half-empty crowd's does. That's an important finding. The hippocampus, a sea-horse structure located just behind your ears, is involved in a wide variety of cognitive functions, including memory. My guess is that dopamine levels are affected, too. These seniors avoid the trap of what would otherwise turn out to be a self-fulfilling prophecy."

Bernard Beckett

"Human spirit is the ability to face the uncertainty of the future with curiosity and optimism. It is the belief that problems can be solved; differences resolved. It is a type of confidence. And it is fragile. It can be blackened by fear and superstition."

Jess Lane

"Optimists have been found in most circumstances to be better equipped to cope with life. They remain positive and steadfast, believing that no matter what, the future is bright with promise and hope."

Mohsin Hamid

Optimism isn't that I'll live forever; optimism is, in the face of a recognized temporary life, I can still find beauty and meaning and connection and something worthwhile."

Robin Cogan

"My optimism is informed by a relentless pursuit of caring for children and families with complex health and social needs. Investing in the health, safety and well-being of community gives me hope that the seeds we plant today will bloom given a rich soil of compassion, nurturing, relationship building and belief in the promise each generation brings."

Cassandra Goodman

"What makes me optimistic is that more and more leaders are realising that successful business transformation is dependent on the extent to which they themselves have the courage to embark on their own personal journey of transformation and exploration"

Victor Perton

Victor Matison was my uncle, a table tennis champion and an eternal optimist. Delivering his eulogy, I referred to his lifelong optimism and quoted his favourite poem:

If you think you are beaten, you are;
If you think you dare not, you don't.
If you'd like to win, but you think you can't,
It is almost a certain - you won't.

If you think you'll lose, you've lost;
For out in this world we find
Success begins with a fellow's will
It's all in the state of mind.

If you think you're outclassed, you are;
You've got to think high to rise.
You've got to be sure of yourself before
You can ever win the prize.

Life's battles don't always go
To the stronger or faster man;
But sooner or later the man who wins
Is the one who thinks he can!

Joseph S. Nye, former Dean of the Kennedy School of Government at Harvard University

"Remember, in the words of the song, the best things in life are free: a kind word; a gentle kiss from someone you love; a slanting shaft of afternoon sunlight coming in the window; a green shoot in Spring; a snowflake on your sleeve in Winter. All you have to do is remember to slow down and smell the flowers."

Pete Jensen

"For me, cultivating optimism begins with humility, recognising that I can't be in control of everything, and trusting that things will work themselves out.

"This act of surrender reduces anxiety and fear and frees up my creativity, hope and energy to take the actions I need for the things over which I do have control, thus making things possible.

"Lived optimism then, is a conscious daily and momentary ritual, that we all can share and pass on to those we lead."

Aminah Georgiou

"Optimism is looking at every situation that you encounter in your life, be it good or bad, as a learning experience. Each experience presents itself as an advantage to move forward."

Glenn Buesnel-May, Leadership Expert

"I was presented with a multitude of challenging life experiences from my earliest years. Somehow, I chose a mind-set that oriented me towards the future of possibility, of hope and ultimately, optimism. For me, it was not the phenomena of 'overcoming' challenges, but to a degree, riding them out and having faith in the oft-forgotten fact that challenges will come and a new day inevitably dawns. And it's this 'new day' that contains endless opportunity to change your lived reality. It can sometimes sound trite, but every future second of our lives gives us the 'second chance'. And it's an optimistic mind-set, partly in anticipation of that positive future of possibility, that allows us to rest on that assurance of the second chance; that opens up a new door to a new reality that defies yesterday's challenges. In contrast, especially for me, if I was pessimistic, I would have simple grown into a vessel of accumulated fear with no faculty for productive change or positive expectation. And unfortunately, it's that type of orientation that leads us to all kinds of dysfunction both individually and socially. I was lucky that as a very young child, I chose optimism over closing the door to growth and betterment by being shackled by fear. Optimism lies in the future path; a path of opportunity, of change, whereas pessimism paints that future palette with a darkness, devoid of the light of meaning and passion-driven purpose. Pessimism is driven by fear and embedded in the negative experiences of our pasts. That's why it's important to reconcile our failures and hardships (past) with the endless opportunities ahead of us (future)."

Professor Lisa Bortolotti, University of Birmingham

"The belief that was optimistically-biased to start with will become more and more realistic over time, because I am ready to change myself in order to change the outcome of my efforts, practising until I actually become a better driver and my chances of success increase. Optimism is never a guarantee of success, but it can become a self-fulfilling prophecy. Isn't that what agency is all about, intervening on ourselves and our environment to make the world closer to how we'd like it? Sounds like a good life to me."

Janelle Bruland, Author

"Optimism changes your outlook, actions, and results."

"Choosing an optimistic mindset is a choice. It's a choice that takes work and means not looking at problems as insurmountable, but rather as opportunities."

Peter Adamis, Writer

"Throughout life, I have found that optimism can be a product of hope, positive reinforcement, life skills, knowledge, experience and a positive outlook on life. Optimism is a driver, an encourager and one of the characteristics of leadership"

James Montgomery, Chief Executive Officer at AFL SportsReady

"For me I've always been what I would call a reflective optimist... time makes me see things more optimistically, you face adversity, you experience difficult circumstances, things look bleak, people's behaviour impacts on you and others, you have the "if only" moments ...if only they had done this, if only they had thought of that, if only they knew this had already happened, if only.. if only.... Optimism always sounds like an easy choice - something you are born with - I'm a ..... "glass is half full" sort of guy. The choice appears like a simple dichotomy - given a choice who would be pessimistic when they can be optimistic? To move from a pessimistic experience or response to a more optimistic view is a habit and for some a skill, learned or innate. I believe everyone starts as a good person, they make decisions along the way, they have experiences, they learn and value different things. Everything we do to others is a behaviour, we are a product of our experience and what we have learnt. And that's where I end up, I unpack everything, I process, I accept difference, I try and make sense of why things happen and when I do my pessimism subsides, my optimism grows, my stress washes away. I smile and I breathe, capable of taking the next step, optimistically."

Voices for Hanging Out with Optimistic People

Meghan Markle, Duchess

"it's so important to surround yourself with people who are grounded and really optimistic."

"True North" Professor Bill George, Harvard Business School

"I am optimistic because I believe in the inherent goodness of people and I am surrounded with positive optimistic people. What a blessing!"

Laura Kuhar, CSIRO

"I was always told to think positively and to stick around positive people, so optimism is mostly a state of mind for me. Sometimes though, optimism is a choice - it is not always easy to find an element of good in the worst situations, but it is possible, even if I have to look really hard!"

Dr Wendy Patrick

"We are drawn to people who make us feel happy, hopeful, and optimistic, and when they are gone, we want to see them again."

Mary Berry, Communities of Respect

"What makes me optimistic? Being surrounded by amazing people who work selflessly to help others and pave futures of opportunity, inclusion, resilience and strength within our communities."

Sharyn County, **Head Of Procurement at Jemena**

"What makes me optimistic is people: Meeting, working with and leading passionate, motivated people. Seeing those I lead and have led be successful and creating a safe environment that takes into account the differences in people to enable this."

Gönül Serbest, Chief Executive Officer, Global Victoria

"Optimism is magnetic - anything is possible when you attract positive energy and people through the right mindset."

Louise Scott Heatley, IACCM

"Striving to see the positive, surrounding myself with like-minded people and being grateful for all that I have makes my life so much happier and more optimistic than ever!"

Anil Dash, CEO of Glitch

"If you can trust in a community, and you can trust in your ability to express yourself, and you can trust in having a safe place to share your ideas, that gives you space to be optimistic,. It gives you space to have some hope to think you have something to share when the ground is shifting under you and you can't take people at their word."

Bedros Keuilian, Fit Body Boot camp

“Only share your big dreams, ambitions, and goals with the people in your life who are positive, optimistic, and have similar ambitions. Those are the people who will encourage, motivate, and inspire you to become the best version of yourself.”

Maria Govers

“I like being optimistic and being surrounded by optimism. Optimism creates positive energy and inspires me to find solutions and opportunities. As a leader, I find myself using positive energy created by my optimism to inspire, lead the way and make work fun empowering the team to find solutions and opportunities."

Voices for Gratitude and Optimism

Paul Levins

"Optimism relies on gratitude. And gratitude is refreshed by optimism."

Professor Oliver Jones, Associate Dean, RMIT

"For me, optimism is being grateful for all the things you do have rather than all the things you don't; and for all the times you succeeded rather than when things went wrong. If you always think you are going to fail, then you probably will, but if you think positively and learn from setbacks rather than get distracted by them, then the sky really is the limit."

Rae Snape, Headteacher

"Gratitude opens one's heart and makes one appreciate the minutiae and detail of life. This openness is the foundation to spotting opportunity and this is the foundation to optimism."

Dr Freya MacMillan

"Gratitude makes me optimistic. Every day I wake, I am thankful. I am grateful for my health, my beautiful family and the opportunities that I've been so fortunate to have. I lost my brother when I was 19, he was only 21. He was healthy and happy but didn't get very long here. For these reasons, I am optimistic in all that I do. I will make sure I live my life to the full in memory of those that did not get the chance."

Louisa Keck

"What makes me optimistic are finding the small pockets of kindness and good in day to day life. Appreciating the moments that make me smile and the ones that take my breath away. Feeling gratitude for the people in my life and excited about the life I get to create with them."

Chris Reddy, Leadership Coach

"What makes me optimistic? It's pretty simple. It's all about appreciating the small things, accepting the setbacks, grasping opportunities and being grateful for the family and friends in my life."

Tony Holmwood

"Rather than being consumed by problems, an optimist views the world through a completely different lens, one focused on exploring opportunity. An optimist expresses gratitude often."

Elaine Ingalls, Journalist

"I believe that optimism is a choice even when things aren't working out in your favor. Having an attitude of gratitude makes it easier to get through the challenging tasks of daily life and difficult seasons."

Pablo Cilotta, IACCM

"My optimism and happiness are enhanced through expressing gratitude and being passionate when learning new things, meeting new people, building relationships based on trust, confidence and building bridges."

Sally Branson, Director at The Suite Set

"For me, optimism has been passed down from my grandmother to my mother. My mum is relentlessly positive, and it is a lovely family trait. Is it nature or nurture people ask? I say - Optimism is a habit, a learned behaviour. Optimism is a choice and a daily practice that stems from being grateful."

Diane Kilkenny, IACCM

"What makes me optimistic? That random acts of human kindness come from the places you least expect them at the times you need them most!"

Voices for Courage and Optimism

A.M. Lewis, Author

"I have MS, and it makes me optimistic to tell myself daily that sadness is a choice, so choose not to live in it. Be optimistic. It's okay to get down, to cry, but don't stay there too long."

Steve Gross, Life is Good Kids Foundation

"I'm an optimist by default. There's no use being pessimistic, it wouldn't work anyway. Optimism to me is the most effective way to deal with adversity. Our survival depends on our ability to find opportunities amidst the obstacles."

Deborah Spratling

"Optimism for me is hoping that whatever life throws at me I have the ability to bounce back from it. I recognise that I have the choice on how I interpret a situation or experience and that old early conditioned self-critical and self-defeating thoughts, no longer have any hold or power over me. I choose now to be kinder and more self-compassionate."

Craig Townsend

"I believe that optimism is key in overcoming hardships. I also believe very strongly in the power of an empathetic response to counsel others and optimism is an element in giving hope to those in need."

Liliane Grace, Author

"An optimistic person is not blindly positive, not someone who denies the difficult side of life; an optimistic person fully recognises life's challenges and still holds that there is a silver lining and an outcome that serves all concerned."

Dave Bartholomay

"I'm an optimist that understands there will indeed be failures—we don't live in a fantasy land. But we can learn from our failures, and optimists believe that success will inevitably follow those failures."

Wah Chin Boon, Neuroendocrinologist, The Florey

"This phrase keeps me optimistic, 'Everything will be alright in the end. If it is not alright, it is not the end.'"

Tony Harding

"Embracing optimism and strength of will over adversity can be a game-changer for us and our colleagues - to enable us to achieve our goals in life. I recommend we embrace optimism champions and role models as part of our journey in life."

Michelle Gielan, Author of Broadcasting Happiness

"In the field of positive psychology, we define optimism as the expectation of good things to happen and the belief that behavior matters, especially in the face of challenges"

Sally James, Author

"Some people are optimistic the sun will come out when deluged with rain; others that there will be rain when the ground is parched; and some that there will be snow just because of its simple beauty. We all have different reasons for having optimism, and sometimes finding it requires greater effort than others. Optimism is what is there waiting for us to dig from sometimes the deepest depths within us enabling us to rise with hope each new day when faced with hopelessness. It is what gives us courage to face each day, and believe that, even if all we do is bring a smile to a sad face, a note of cheer to someone who is struggling, then nothing is wasted. Optimism is believing that life can always be better, that, when facing a wall too high to climb, there will be a door to find. Optimism is allowing ourselves to be nourished by the contributions of those around us, that there is always room to grow and improve, and that if we believe that goodness is what pervades our hearts and actions, then we will conquer adversity."

Denise Avchen, Environmental Research Advocates

"Optimism is the grease in the wheels of progress. It's what enables us to move forward with all personal, professional or societal change. It's the element needed to make dreams come true. In my mind, optimism and courage are synonymous, beautiful and essential to life"

Dr Klaus Vella Bardon

"Each one of us is called to take a stand. Even everyday and apparently simple decisions have an impact on the way we are generous, compassionate, fair and positive so as to encourage optimism and hope in a world that too easily yields to being cynical and defeatist."

Ernest Shackleton, Explorer

"Optimism is true moral courage"

Denise Allen

"Optimism is the light in one's heart and mind that brings joy and purpose into our lives. But without having the courage of your convictions, principles, ethics, tolerance, compassion and love for others this light will only flicker and eventually fade"

Muneera Bano, Swinburne University of Technology[1]

"Optimism is what keeps you to continue your journey even when you can't see your destination. There will be ups and downs, but in the end, how you react to those moments will define your success when you eventually reach your destination."

Voices for Resilience and Optimism

Professor Jane Burns

"People talk about tenacity and resilience and strength of character but it is optimism that drives behaviour when on some days it would be easier to say "stop - I give up, it's too hard. Optimism is believing in the impossible and then taking the steps to make it possible."

Chris Norman, CEO, Goulburn Broken Catchment Management Authority

"The need for optimism has never been more important in dealing with the whole set of daily and long-term complex problems. Our resilience journey has been strengthened by an understanding of the critical need for optimism to underpin our approaches."

Emily Jaksch

"Everyone faces adversity but it's how you deal with it that defines the person. Your levels of optimism underpin your resilience and successful response to that adversity!"

Diana Hodgson, Dynamic Global HR Leader

"Leadership – the case for optimism? People want to be inspired! Given the future of work and the reality and pace of change as it evolves, optimism is an important trait to keep us moving productively forward. Resilience is its companion. As I see it, being an optimist doesn't mean that you can't see faults and flaws, but it means that you see them as obstacles to be overcome and gives a language and anchor from which to draw the energy to move forward."

Robert Moritz, Global Chair, PwC

"Embracing resilience fundamentally means building an optimism in people that will allow them to see failure as a step toward greater knowledge. I believe building organizational resilience and the ability to adapt to unforeseen circumstances is rising to the top of the business agenda, particularly given the challenges we're seeing in the 21st century"

Matt Joski, Sheriff, Kewaunee County

"Optimism is the engine that powers resiliency. While there are many character strengths which we all possess, they are all deficient unless supported by and deeply rooted in Optimism. We are impacted in everything from personal relationships to physical health by the existence or absence of Optimism. This powerful trait is not one founded in the denial of reality or refusal of circumstances, but rather the unyielding belief that even our darkest hours bring with them hope and empowerment."

Dr Krystal Evans

"Optimism is empowering. It's the belief that no matter what challenges you face, that you can make a difference. That your voice and your actions matter. It underpins resilience, determination and ambition"

April Chepovskygold, Lawyer and Entrepreneur

"The Case for Optimism? Belief in self and dreams inspires others to be the same....Resiliency. You cannot inspire others with negativity."

Renee Branson, Author

"Optimism is the fuel and the faith that drives our resilience when our other resilience tools (reason, composure, vision) are temporarily out of reach. Optimism is the chair we sink into that we know will hold us until reason and composure catch up."

Libby Mears, CEO, Leisure Networks

"I am optimistic when I see the strength of communities who have overcome adversity, seeing people included who are usually excluded and when I see people willing to display gentleness, empathy, compassion and kindness."

Dr Emily Edwards, Immunologist

"Being optimistic gives you the resilience and power to overcome life's challenges empowering you to live, learn, lead and ultimately make a difference to the lives of others."

Emily Esfahani Smith, Author of The Power of Meaning

"Far from being delusional or faith-based, having a positive outlook in difficult circumstances is not only an important predictor of resilience—how quickly people recover from adversity—but it is *the* most important predictor of it. People who are resilient tend to be more positive and optimistic compared to less-resilient folks; they are better able to regulate their emotions; and they are able to maintain their optimism through the most trying circumstances.

"This is what Dr. Dennis Charney, the dean of Mount Sinai School of Medicine, found when he examined approximately 750 Vietnam war veterans who were held as prisoners of war for six to eight years. Tortured and kept in solitary confinement, these 750 men were remarkably resilient. Unlike many fellow veterans, they did not develop depression or posttraumatic stress disorder after their release, even though they endured extreme stress. What was their secret? After extensive interviews and tests, Charney found ten characteristics that set them apart. The top one was optimism. The second was altruism. Humor and having a meaning in life—or something to live for—were also important."

Editorial Board, Cape Gazette

"The thing about optimism, however, is the inherent sense that no matter how bad things are, people have the resilience, determination and intelligence to seek and find solutions."

Sarah Norton

"Looking at this from a more personal perspective, I believe a person's optimism is heavily influenced by relationships forged, past achievements and hurdles overcome. As these experiences lead to personal growth in many areas and perhaps increased resilience, it may enable one to feel more prepared and confident knowing they are able to handle whatever challenge they may face, whether consciously chosen or unexpected, and therefore be more optimistic of the future regardless of what is happening in the world. Basis - personal experience."

Chris Botha, Economic Development Professional

"Optimistic leadership starts with a choice, a choice everyone is given every time they walk into their office, workplace, home, sports ground, cultural venue or public space. That choice is to always engage with your fellow humans with a real curiosity and interest. Always remind yourself that everyone else has many stories to tell and by listening and engaging with those stories we make them realise that they have a narrative and a purpose. It encourages them and makes them believe in themselves. Their stories also make your own life more interesting; it makes you realise the capabilities and resilience of the people around you and it also makes you more confident about what you are capable of."

Voices for Love and Optimism

Morni Chen, The Future of Power

"We have a choice between fear and love. Optimism is an expression of love, a higher energy and so it is more powerful than fear."

Vitaly Geyman

What makes me optimistic is that I always believed that deep inside most of us know that love trumps fear."

Sneha Ayyagari, Schneider Sustainable Energy Fellow, Natural Resources Defense Council

"Optimism is a source of strength and peace. It fuels the hope needed to see challenges as opportunities for learning and helps us to lead our lives more intentionally with love."

Judy Rodgers, President, Images & Voices of Hope

"It is the nature of the human spirit to express love, peace and joy. We do drift from our true nature in some moments, but time and truth ultimately call us back to who we really are, which is the deepest rationale for optimism."

Michael Kawula, CEO of Dinner Table MBA

"Optimism is a non-biased mindset, obtainable by all, that when turned on, defeats life's inevitable obstacles and opens up opportunities that can make all live and love life!"

Professor Vijay Varadharajan, Global Innovation Chair in Cyber Security

"The cornerstone of my optimism comes from the power of love and will that make ordinary people do extraordinary things."

Voices for Optimism and Health

Dr Carol Graham, Leo Pasvolsky senior fellow, Brookings Institution

"The link between optimism and longevity is strong."

Catherine Barrett, Director of Celebrate Ageing.

"Optimism is essential to healthy ageing and longevity. Research shows that people who internalise ageism or only think about their ageing as loss, live on average 7 years less than those who are optimistic and think about the positive aspects of their ageing. Optimism enables people to act in ways that are empowered – to continue to throw themselves into life with enthusiasm."

Pollyanna Lenkic, Leadership Expert and Coach

"Optimism connects us to a more constructive place both emotionally and physically. We see potential rather than obstacles."

Jessica Stillman

"Optimistic expectations about aging actually help us age happily and healthily."

Suzanne Segerstrom

"People who are optimistic are more committed to their goals, are more successful in achieving their goals, are more satisfied with their lives, and have better mental and physical health when compared to more pessimistic people"

Lisa Bortolotti

"Optimistic beliefs are good for our relationships and our health, even when they are not backed up by evidence, if they make us more resilient and resourceful agents"

Danielle Guttman-Klein

"Optimism is truly the answer to so much of what is going on around the world. The direct correlation between optimism and successful cancer treatment is becoming more real and scientifically proven, Beyond all that, optimism makes life a better journey."

Jessica Cassity

"Optimists Feel Healthier: If you think that the world is inherently good, and that life will work out in your favor, you're more likely to rate your own health and sense of well-being as better."

Monique Tello, MD

"Optimism is as much as skill as a personality trait. You can train your brain to recognize and counteract negative thinking — your heart and health will be better for it."

MindUP™

"Choosing to view life optimistically can increase our brain capacity! It relaxes our amygdala, creates chemical balance in our brains, and allows our prefrontal cortex to take charge"

Steve Anderson, Chief Executive Officer, The University of Kansas Health System Campus

"I'm an optimist by nature. No pessimist gets anywhere. It's a dead road. So optimism is key in health care. People need to feel that positive energy."

Margaret H. Greenberg, coauthor "Profit from the Positive"

"Don't underestimate the power of a good night's sleep. Remember optimism isn't the glass half-full; it is how we interpret both good and challenging events."

Voices for Optimism at Work

Sally Foley-Lewis

"Bringing more optimism into workplaces aligns with improving workplace cultures that lead to less staff-turnover, higher productivity and profits. Optimism can start from reframing an attitude or viewpoint from mistrust or concern to most people want to do well and most people want to get along, be engaged and be a valuable contributor. Keeping this in mind as we communicate, drive a strategic vision, check progress on implementing a plan, means that if you see an error or something is not clear, start from that more optimistic stance and ask questions to uncover what's going on."

Diane Hamilton, Creator of the Curiosity Code Index

"Optimism and curiosity are critical for innovative workplaces. That desire to learn and explore provides a rush of creativity. Optimism clears the way for empathy and understanding. Optimism leads to tenacity to see a project through completion and helps us overcome the fear of failure."

Olivia Nambi, President of Generation Bridge (GB), Uganda

"Optimism has contributed to an improvement in labor force skills and digitization giving hope for businesses to thrive over the next decade around the world. I am hopeful that the increased number of optimists will find solutions to other global challenges."

Todd Tucker, The Roosevelt Institute

"In general there's no point in talking if there's not at least some grounds for optimism."

Voices for Strategy and Optimism

Daniel Redman

"Optimism is core to strategy. Optimism drives innovation in any strategy. It is the fundamental source of fire that lights the way for creativity to thrive"

Nina Anderson, Anderson Advisory

"Optimism resides at the core of good strategy, it provides the platform for critical and clear thinking, the ability to challenge embedded knowledge, the humility to ask questions and be open to new ideas. It is also critical for engaging stakeholders and communicating the benefits of the strategy.

"Optimism is essential throughout implementation too, without it you'll bring the wrong energy and will be less inclined to motivate others, embrace new initiatives and adapt to market changes."

Dr Asaf Bitton

"I believe in optimism as a strategic imperative."

Allan Shaw, Principal, Knox School

"Strategy is about envisioning and planning for a better future. Without optimism there is little point in planning for a better future."

Nóirín Mosley, CEO, Race Party

"I believe strategy and optimism are intrinsically linked and co-dependent. If you aren't optimistic about your strategy how can it achieve your desired outcome?"

Paul Pastulovic , Divisional Manager, Yarra Valley Water

"Strategy and optimism go hand in hand, a good strategy has its roots in optimism. When you are building for the future, if you don't have a level of optimism in what you are doing, you can miss opportunities that can present themselves"

Adam Bowcutt, Psychologist

"Optimism must be the foundation of strategy because the power of collective confidence helps create sustained energy and momentum. Consistent high performance is a result of an optimistic and purposeful vision of the future."

David Pich, Chief Executive of the Institute of Managers and Leaders Australia & New Zealand

"I have a relatively simple view that strategy and optimism go hand in hand. A leader arrives at a strategy via a process of consultation, investigation and analysis. The strategy that is selected is selected because it is – all things being equal – the best strategy for a given situation. It is, therefore, by definition, a positive process and a positive outcome. Even if the strategy itself doesn't appear to be 'positive' – it is the best approach at the time for the business, team or organisation. So, I consider optimism and sound strategy to be highly correlated. In short, a leader creates the strategy, and she needs to own that strategy and be accountable for it. It's her strategy, and she needs to be optimistic that it will work."

Jeff Kerr-Bell

Successful strategy cannot exist without optimism! Strategy is the act of navigating through challenges towards something better and you cannot envision or define better without being optimistic that it indeed exists! Therefore, no optimism =no strategy!

David Sharrock, author of Fighting for Enterprise Success: through the eye of the tiger.

"With business strategy itself, optimism needs to underpin and influence strategic direction and planning. Setting a strategic direction that will enable a business to stand out in the marketplace from all others in the same industry is premised on hope, namely, hope for a better future for the business as it works to its competitive advantage. It then takes the formation and implementation of planning to enable the overall strategy to work. The mindset of a leader and team members alike is essential here. There is no room for half-belief when they are working to an agreed strategy. There is no point in them setting goals and plans with a negative mindset while contemplating failure and envisaging defeat. They must envisage the end result and work wholeheartedly toward its achievement, full of hope, and sharing an optimism that all their efforts will be successful in the end. Their optimism must not be disingenuous. It must be grounded in reality and tested against milestones, reassuring them that good progress is being made.

"When it comes to good business strategy, hope fuels optimism, just like a match lights a fire, while optimism acts like oxygen, keeping the flames alight."

Chris Reddy, Leadership Coach

"A good strategy requires clear goals and aspirations, which by default is future focused optimism. Successful strategies rely on commitment, momentum and support from others. Bringing these together using a collaborative approach with strong values and positivity, only enhances long term strategic outcomes."

Richard Hames, Futurist

"If optimism and hope are at the core of strategy conversations, the strategy can result in levels of engagement, inspiration and trust that are both powerful and inimitable."

Ken Sterling

"As a way of life, business strategy, or leadership philosophy, optimism will serve you well in the good times and the bad."

Louka Parry, Education Changemakers

"Make a positive culture your key strategy. The benefits are overwhelming, and as a positive and optimistic leader you are not only enabling others to do their best work but to live fuller lives"

Pip Marlow

"History is still being written. Optimism is a strategy to make our history a better one."

Jim Rohrbach, Leadership Coach

"Optimism is the ONLY strategy if you want to be successful. How many naysayers have made a difference in the world?"

Anne Scottlin

“Optimism is the ability to occupy the present with equanimity and aplomb, a practical strategy since our future will soon become our present in any case”

Mick Farrell, CEO of Resmed

"Optimism is the triumph of hope over fear, of truth over deception, but it must be grounded in reality. Optimism without realism is just a dream; hope alone is not a strategy. Detailed planning of scenarios, laying out of plans towards an ambitious goal, and then inspiring a team to climb that hill together with passion and a mission greater than oneself – that combination is a sure path to success."

Ash Hamer, Yarra Valley Water

"Without optimism in a strategy, there is no hope of excellence. Optimism in a strategy provides enthusiasm and drive, but this should always be tempered with a touch of realism."

Noam Chomsky

"Optimism is a strategy for making a better future. Because unless you believe that the future can be better, you are unlikely to step up and take responsibility for making it so."

Professor Colin Jevons, Course Director, Monash University Bachelor of Business

"A strategy without optimism is doomed to fail - by definition! Any plan to influence the future must be optimistic."

Kieran Flanagan

"What makes us optimistic is action. Hope is a great thing to sell, but it's a poor personal strategy, whereas optimism is earned through focus and is a far more reliable predictor of success"

Wendy Born

"I think optimism is the foundation for developing and achieving a good strategy. With an optimistic leadership team, they are more likely to develop an ambitious strategy and then feel more confident about achieving the actions to deliver it. Their optimism also flows down throughout their respective teams, which has flow-on impacts to engagement, productivity and safety."

Dr Parag Shirnamé

“Optimism is the powerful understory that helps leaders to stand tall above the industry canopy. Mixed with a strategic buy-in by the team into the overall plan, optimism from the leader can be a major motivator for the team members. Clarity in each member’s role in jointly achieving the results is paramount. It doesn’t take much. A simple acknowledgement by the leader can galvanize the team to work miracles.”

Darren Woolley

"As a business leader, optimism keeps you turning up and trying even when the odds are against you. Like Steven Bradbury, Australia's Olympic Speed Skating Gold Medalist, success comes from being there to take advantage of the opportunities as they present themselves. This is not just luck, but a deliberate strategy when you are being out-spent and out-resourced by the competition."

Natalie Foeng, CFO, Yarra Valley Water

"Optimism is a critical enabler of growth, new opportunities and sustainable business. We are now at a turning point with strategy, where our days of surviving purely on profit and risk mitigation are numbered. Optimism is ultimately what will keep our businesses sustainable."

Miriam Feiler, co-founder, bizzi.co

"Creating and implementing a good strategy is based solely on the end result we seek. The result inevitably involves a strong desire to win, prevail, succeed. The road to success is littered with missteps, mistakes and failures that can easily derail you. What is needed is optimism. Optimism is a muscle. Without it, you will not have the push-through to overcome seemingly insurmountable setbacks to stick to your game plan and see your strategy through to successful completion."

Voices for Innovation and Optimism

Dr Martin Parkinson AC PMC, former Secretary, Australian Department of the Prime Minister and Cabinet

“Optimism drives curiousity which in turn fosters innovation and invention. So whatever the challenges we face, it’s better to tackle them with an optimistic bent, confident that nothing is insurmountable given enough will and effort.”

Cecilia Hilder, Institute for Culture and Society

"We can’t have innovation without optimism - hope and confidence about the future. We now think of innovation in economic terms - about the wealth it will create - but innovation is creativity, it is doing and believing in making life better. Innovation is, in turn, optimism. We all have moments where it is hard to be optimistic, but those of us who have had very difficult things happen know that things get better. It is our obligation to show those around us the truth and the power of optimism."

Brad Roberts, Xinova

"Optimism is the core of innovation: that there’s a better way"

Chris Reddy, Leadership Coach

"All innovation, change and progress must come from a belief that things can improve for the better. Innovation requires change. Change is not possible without optimism and the idea that we can overcome obstacles and challenges."

Lisa Chikarovski

"Optimism drives us to look at the 'solution' in the context of a 'problem' - it changes the negative connotation of 'problematic' into an opportunity to think about how we can do better. Striving to improve is the underlying driver of innovation - the desire to make the world a better place."

Evan Shellshear, Author of Bestseller Innovation Tools

"The driving force behind disruptive innovation is a belief in the possible, a belief in progress, a belief in something better. "The Case for Optimism" embodies this disruptive perspective and gives us the mindset and drive to achieve it."

Oludotun Babayemi, co-founder of Nigeria's Connected Development

"Optimism drives imagination, with it, we exist, without it, we become inexistent."

Robert Noyce, Intel's Co-Founder

"Optimism is an essential ingredient of innovation. How else can the individual welcome change over security, adventure over staying in safe places?"

Dona Tantirimudalige

"Where necessity might be the mother of invention, without optimism, invention would seldom grow beyond the embryonic. What do I mean by that? Well, I believe optimism is critical in every step towards innovation. The drive to dream of what might be possible unconstrained by the perceived restrictions of the status quo requires optimism. The courage to not only envision the future you want but to step into planning and creating that future requires optimism. The willingness to step away from the theoretical and into action requires optimism. And when facing failure, the resilience to dust yourself off, regroup, learn, and try again (or try something different) requires optimism. Every step towards innovation requires optimism."

Dr KH Kim

Want to Innovate? Science Says, "Be Optimistic!"

Associate Professor Kate Fox, RMIT

"Optimism is having the security to fail on your own terms knowing that you will be backed in despite the outcome."

"I believe optimism is the sparkle in our world. It is the optimists that believe positive change IS possible; they are the innovators, pioneers and changemakers that persist and continuously work towards a more positive world."

Melis Senova, Author of "This Human"

"We are creative beings and have the ability to change our perceptions of reality just by changing our minds. If we are optimistic in our mindset, we perceive our reality positively, which then encourages us to go about creating more of it."

Paul Ramadge, Managing Director, The PLuS Alliance

"To dream, to imagine, to think about the world in new ways, to set out to make a positive difference, and to inspire others to join you . . . herein is the essence of optimism and innovation. Here's to the thousands of exceptional leaders who embody this spirit."

Paul Pastulovic

"The relationship between optimism and innovation is perfectly summed up in the line from the Frank Sinatra song Love and Marriage... 'you can't have one without the other'"

Entrepreneurship and Optimism

Chris Gale, CEO of Latin Resources

"As an entrepreneur, you have to be an eternal optimist!"

T. Boone Pickins, American Entrepreneur

"A good plan and hard work helped me get there, but neither are possible without healthy optimism. So, be the eternal optimist."

Miriam Feiler, co-founder, bizzi.co

Optimism drives every entrepreneur. The deep belief that we can, and will "make it", whatever our "it" is, enables us to push through the obstacles. Optimism helps us believe that our next venture will thrive, even after a spectacular fall. In this way, you could argue that 'small business' isn't actually the engine the powers most economies in the world. It is Optimism."

Jonathan Lamb, CEO, The Entrepreneurs' Forum

"Entrepreneurs are all about resilience and optimism and taking on and overcoming challenges and they are the key to creating future jobs and prosperity."

Mariano Fabrizio, Partner, Nicholson y Cano Abogados

"Optimism is a state of mind that works as the underlying asset of every project, the main pillar of every successful enterprise."

Dr Andreas Kappes and Dr Tali Sharot

"Entrepreneurs are more optimist than the average person. Is being an optimist a helpful thing for entrepreneurs and innovators?... It turns out optimism can be a blessing and a curse. Optimism enhances the likelihood of identifying creative solutions. It also induces over-confidence in the ability to successfully implement these solutions, which makes it more likely that entrepreneurs will take the plunge. It also makes entrepreneurs more persistent in the face of setbacks, protects against stress and makes networking easier."

Richard Branson, Entrepreneur

"Those swimming in a glass half empty are more likely to drown than those swimming in a glass half full. I'm an incurable optimist, and I like it that way. It's enabled me to remain hopeful and future-focused. Attitude is everything in life and in business."

Susan Bibby

"As a farmer and budding entrepreneur, for me optimism lies in investing new innovative renewable technologies in production of clean green environmentally sustainable foods, so that as a country we are self-sufficient. I'm talking about food security. Following years of challenge and markets that are heavily influenced by overseas players I believe Australia has an optimistic future if they begin to start with looking after their own first and with this they showcase inexpensive innovative food production technologies for our own populations rather than selling our commodities continually overseas."

Michelle Worthington, Author

"I am optimistic when I see creative entrepreneurs. People with creative minds are valued in a whole range of businesses as this can translate into fantastic writing skills, unique concepts and new, strategic and efficient ways of doing things. Many skills can be learnt over time, but it is exceedingly difficult to teach creativity. Our society is learning to value an imaginative, creative thinker."

Stephen Ibaraki, Futurist and Entrepreneur

"In collecting more than 200 attributes that define success with entrepreneurs, there are four that stand out—one is optimism. When looking at the related area of happiness, prior to 2000, it was believed that people were born with a happiness set point—immutable thus setting your course for the future. However, when studying Tibetan monks and their brain activity, it was discovered that this could be raised through technique. The same is true of Optimism; you can increase your optimism by reframing everything into opportunities or key lessons for growth. This is similar to stress hormones, they are produced in relation to how you frame workload and challenges—think optimistically about opportunities and skill growth—the stress levels go down thus improving your life quality. Finally, there is this definition of success related to Grit most recently defined by psychologist Angela Duckworth which I'm modifying based upon my experiences:

Talent x hyper effort = skill

Skill x hyper effort = achievement

Achievement x passion x perseverance x optimism (squared) = Grit applied over long-term goals = Success"

Nick Stanley, CEO of Runway

"It's been my experience that optimism is the single-most-important characteristic of the successful entrepreneur. It's a characteristic that you look for in the toughest of times."

Nancy Youseff, Author of "Fear Money Purpose."

"The way I see it, entrepreneurs are typically a different breed: we don't think the same as everyone else. We are eternally optimistic, even in the fast of overwhelmingly difficult odds. That optimism creates the ideas that keep you persistent, resilient and bouncing back when things fail. It's almost like a disease!

"Having a positive outlook for the future and for the world as a whole makes entrepreneurs the visionaries that they are. When you're optimistic, you're usually a happier person and that creates endorphins, also known as the happy hormones.

"But I think the biggest thing about entrepreneurs being over-optimistic is it means that they're very focused on achieving their goals – which makes them super clear on their strategy. If you're optimistic and driven and you can get buy-in from the people around you, particularly your teams and key stakeholders, and that can show a stronger leadership style and inform your strategy."

Science, Technology and Optimism

Michael Nelson, Public Policy at Cloudflare

"I remain VERY optimistic about technology (and the scientists and engineers who create and apply it) and very pessimistic about politics (and particularly that subspecies of politician that holds back technology and progress to protect narrow special interests)."

Sheryl Sandberg, Chief Operating Officer, Facebook

"Technologists have always been optimists. We're optimists because we have to be. If you want to do something that has never been done before, so many people will tell you it cannot be done."

Nicola Watkinson, Austrade Senior Trade and Investment Commissioner for North America

"I remain optimistic about the impact disruptive technologies will have on the way in which we work and live. It would be easy to believe that new technology will lead to a loss of opportunity for many people. Yet new inventions have been displacing human labor for many years and they have led to a growth in employment and new job opportunities. There are many characteristics of humans that cannot be replaced by machines like creativity, intuition and empathy. By having people work with machines there is the potential to create great new strides forward and address some problems which have seemed intractable until now."

Alison Rowe, Chair of the Future Business Council

"Our energy market is experiencing a transition like no other. As we move to decentralized sustainable energy grid, we must ensure we balance the environmental, social and economic impacts. This transition creates amazing opportunities for the future business of our world through the alignment of technology and energy, whilst giving ownership of energy back to the people. I'm an optimist and have surrounded myself with action-driven optimistic people to provide more opportunity to all and especially those who are disadvantaged."

Bradley Deacon, Advisor, PrivacyShell Corp

"The Fourth Industrial no doubt the technology Revolution, is our fourth revolution and like its predecessors, will create a range of jobs in industries such as IoT, AI and digital technology. It will also create fear like previous revolutions, in particular the industrial revolution, however as we embrace the technology and see its benefits we will adapt to all the good it will bring to society overall and optimism will prevail as to its value."

Elad Gil

"I think fundamentally, optimism is one of those things where the more people believe that you can do great positive things to the world through technology, the more people will and the bigger you'll think."

Warwick Peel, Co-founder, Future Directors Institute

"The case for optimism stems from my belief in robots shaking the life out of us! If the Edelman Trust barometer states 85% don't trust the system and Gallup says that only 15% are thriving at work, then humanity is somewhat dead. Many of us in the western world are asleep at the wheel, we are digital consumers of nonsense, we are often self-driven egos striving for what? We need to better address mindfulness and equip ourselves with the joys of life, to be, not to have. Artificial intelligence will leapfrog those who are not solving real problems and those who are not passionate about purpose, and so the machines and human interaction will harness the rise up for better solutions for our planet and society. My optimism stems from the machines teaching us how to thrive in life again, because A.I and tech-enabled solutions to enormous problems like climate change, health, food security and water scarcity will be in our grasp, we will regain empathy, we will relearn to be."

Professor Stephen Hawking

"Perhaps with the tools of this new technological revolution, we will be able to undo some of the damage done to the natural world by the last one, industrialization. We will aim to finally eradicate disease and poverty. Every aspect of our lives will be transformed...I am an optimist and I believe that we can create AI for the good of the world, that it can work in harmony with us."

Roger Leonard, Community Planning and Development Expert, U.S. Department of Housing and Urban Development

"In the short term, I am not optimistic at all. Politics seems to be Pandora's box which is the wild card as it seems to divide us more everyday... But long-term the future looks bright and very interesting. Robotics will make life easier, and to allow more to leverage their work in ways as unknown to us as the Internet was to my grandfather. Medicine will unlock a better, longer life with health not uncommon into one's 100's. Technology will bring a merging of knowledge and expansion of the mind, allowing us to better understand nature and ourselves. If we can survive each other, we have glimpsed a bright and productive future. But every generation might have also said the same…"

Linny Thom

"The Case for Optimism? Economic change, changing environment, growth industries, introduction of new technologies and planning for the future."

Bryce Vissel, Professor of Neuroscience, UTS

"What makes me optimistic? The possibilities generated by human endeavour. There's definitely a long way to go, and a lot more research to do in spinal cord research and research of the brain. Optimism and belief that science holds the answers underpin everything we do. As we do the hard work, we remain optimistic and thankful to the people who believe in our vision of creating a world where cure is possible for spinal cord injury and brain disorders."

Luci Ellis, Assistant Governor (Economic), Reserve Bank of Australia

"Some of the pessimism about productivity is happening alongside great optimism in some quarters about a new Industrial Revolution built on better algorithms. The truth may well lie somewhere in the middle. It might also take a while to assert itself."

Voices for Climate Optimism

Joyce Msuya, Assistant Secretary-General, United Nations

"I am an eternal, impatient optimist. The environmental challenges we face are daunting but I believe we have the knowledge, ingenuity and tools to transform our planet. We owe it to future generations. In the last year, the state of our environment has been making headline news and young people are on the streets holding us to account. This groundswell of commitment grows each day and I am incredibly optimistic because time and again, humanity has risen to the challenge and I believe we can do so again. As anthropologist Margaret Mead once said, "Never believe that a few caring people can't change the world. For, indeed, that's all who ever have.""

Youssef Nassef, Climate Adaptation Director, UNFCCC

"What makes me optimistic? I believe in the ability of humankind to imminently reverse the degradation of its interface with nature - an imperative condition for our continued existence on Earth."

Jacinda Ardern, PM of New Zealand

"You may well argue that, based on our current trajectory, now is not the time for optimism. "But if we only talk about the loss of glacier mass or sea level rises we run the risk of a society that believes all is lost and that it is simply too late. "It is not. "No one has the luxury of copping out. Not those who deny climate change, nor those who believe it's too far gone. "Now is the time for optimism and for hope and crucially a plan.

Antonio Guterres, Secretary General, United Nations

"The vibrant contributions of regions, cities, businesses and investors, and the fact that the public is engaging with governments makes me optimistic that we can reverse the trends of Climate Change"

Crucke Jean-Luc, Ministre Wallon du Budget

"If you really want to combat climate change, the weapon to use that does not result in fatalities is innovation. Counter pessimism with optimism and intelligence. This fuels innovation."

Bruce Davis, Managing Director of Abundance Investment

"Optimism fuels invention. Optimism fuels change. Optimism finds ways to solve problems. Climate change is a cause that needs optimism."

Imran Ahmad

"Optimism is what keeps us moving, it helps in achieving our goals and a better society. My work on climate change and sustainability is driven by optimism, a sustainable future for all."

Thomas Waitz

"We have to stay optimistic or we won't find solutions to implement the Paris agreement into practical policies. We keep optimistic that we will find solutions"
David Roberts @drvox

"When it comes to climate change, there is no such thing as "game over" or "too late" or "screwed" or "no hope."

Michael Mann

“People ask me how I can possibly be optimistic about prospects for averting dangerous climate change in the face of the obstacles standing in our way. I tell them it's simple. It's all about the re-engagement of young folks we are witnessing today"

David Wallace-Wells

"I don’t believe fear and alarm are the only options; there is a place for hope and optimism."

Boris Johnson, Prime Minister of the UK

"I have always been deeply optimistic about the potential of technology to make the world a better place. If we get this right, future generations will look back on climate change as a problem that we solved by determined global action and the prowess of technology."

Voices for Optimism, Faith and Hope

There is a strong connection between faith and optimism. The Dalai Lama, amongst other faith leaders, is a big fan of optimism.

Janine Kirk

"Without faith we have nothing, without hope there is nothing and without love we are nothing. Optimistic leaders create the conditions where faith, hope and love can thrive."

The Dalai Lama

1. "Choose optimism. It feels better."
2. "Optimism does not mean being blind to the actual reality of a situation. It means maintaining a positive spirit to continue to seek a solution to any given problem. And it means recognizing that any given situation has many different aspects—positive as well as problematic."
3. "I feel optimistic about the future because humanity seems to be growing more mature; scientists are paying more attention to our inner values, to the study of mind and the emotions."

Saint Josemaria Escriva

"Christian optimism is not a sugary optimism, nor is it a mere human confidence that everything will turn out all right. It is an optimism that sinks its roots into an awareness of our freedom, and the sure knowledge of the power of grace."

Sister Jayanti, European Director of the Brahma Kumaris

"Just as nature goes through its cycles, and day will definitely follow the darkest night, although there are many things that feel very dark at the moment, there is a conviction that light will not only penetrate the darkness but banish it - so that the day will begin. Legends and myths of every civilisation have remembered that the power of good ultimately conquers evil. This is the optimism with which I hold a vision for a better world."

Dr Adam Kassam, Chief Resident Physician, Physical Medicine & Rehabilitation at Western University, Canada

"Optimism is the positive distillation of hope. Given the current challenges we face as a global society, optimism will be a vital tool for creative problem solving for current and future generations."

Warren Davies, The Unbreakable Farmer

"Without optimism hope is diminished, the future becomes clouded. No matter the darkness of the days, optimism sheds light on the path leading forward to a brighter future."

Alice Sidhu

"Optimism = Hope. What is there to be hopeful or optimistic about? The fact that we are even thinking about having this conversation. That we can have it freely and openly. That our views are solicited, considered; they don't necessarily have to be embraced or accepted. It's the engagement and dialogue that matters. And more than this? There is constant talk of change and the impact of this on skills, people and organisations......Is our perspective one of challenge or opportunity? Technology can help problems we have been trying to address for so long in health, education and the environment. Recent examples of emergency response in Puerto Rico have helped expedite recovery. Industries are being transformed and it is all being defined with a UX focus. It's coming quickly and can seem overwhelming. We can focus on that or we can think about new ways to learn, access information, develop new skills and deliver and consume services. A little scary, but if it wasn't we wouldn't be trying hard enough."

Jared Mellinger

"The Bible promotes optimism, but it is a certain kind of optimism. It is not the secular optimism of positive thinking or the natural optimism of a laid-back personality, but the godly optimism of Christian hope. True hope endures in the darkness"

Chris Drake, The Mother and Child Health and Education Trust

“As Alexander Pope put it: "Hope springs eternal in the human breast" and if we shut down hope, optimism and trust in goodness we are shutting down an inherent part of what it means to be a human being, i.e. to envision and then move towards a better tomorrow, with head, heart and hands. Having built our castle in the sky we do then have to lay its foundations on the ground in the muddy realities of today but not to aim for it is to condemn ourselves to it never happening.

“This is not to advocate a blind and naive expectation that there will not be setbacks, difficulties and failures or that we should ignore the benefit, prudence and necessity of precaution, planning, a fallback plan B and sometimes some healthy cynicism but. learning as we go along, we must look ahead with a smile, positivity and confidence if we are to have any chance of building the future we want. We might make it and we not make it, but if we don't try we surely won't.

“Pessimism closes the heart and soul, blinkers the eyes and lowers the head. It shuts off dreams and limits the horizon of possibilities. Optimism opens the heart, lightens up and lifts the spirit, boosts morale and stretches our vision to new realms, forging a bridge from an envisaged future, to which our heart soars, back to the present where we can work to make it happen.”

Bojosi Gamontle

"Optimism is hope made alive. It is a decision to exist above negativity and despair. Optimism elevates your imagination to a realm of possibilities. It is in this realm that creativity and motivation bloom, and success becomes a reality"

Christalla Jamil, Headteacher, Eastfield Primary

"By having faith and helping others, my optimism grows because I am thankful. I try to surround myself with positive people, and whatever life throws at me, I seek solutions."

Sister Shivani, Brahma Kumaris

"Unconditional Optimism is the Soul of your Faith"

Riva Levinson

"Optimism comes from hope, which is sustained by faith, and drawn from a belief in God's Plan"

LaMonique Hamilton Barnes

"I believe what God says about me, that I am fearfully and wonderfully made, and He has plans for my prosperity, hope and future. I have no choice but to be optimistic, because I know this life is rigged in my favor!"

Renee Branson, Author

"Optimism, to me, is the belief that the current challenge is neither permanent or pervasive. Optimism does not require me to be cheerful or chipper but it invites me to be hopeful. The most powerful optimism I have felt and witnessed has been through aching tears and white knuckles. Hope and optimism are strong enough to sit with us in our dark places."

Victoria Cope

"Optimism to me is the essence of hope. It's seeing opportunities rather than challenges, visualising a path to success and striving to achieve your full potential. Optimism provides the lens and focus we need, to be our best self every day."

Sue Doherty, Mayor of the City of South Perth

"Faith is the foundation for my optimism"

Tammra Warby, medical practitioner at Coomera on the Gold Coast and Co-author of "The General Practice Exam Handbook."

"Optimism to me turns a complete roadblock into a temporary setback. My case for optimism is that as a living expression of hope for the future, it will pull you through the toughest times of your life. Many times in healthcare and through natural disasters, I have witnessed how optimists respond to the worst thing that has ever happened to them. It is a deeply inspiring and admirable quality to view in action.

"Optimists firstly accept the reality of the situation and immediately begin workshopping the problem to solve it. They always ask, 'What's next?'. Despite how hard it is to practise gratitude through pain, they remain appreciative of all that is still good in their life. Whether facing devastation or illness, the optimist is already planning their adaptation or recovery. In the midst of the darkest times, they still bring their humour to the situation and find the lighter side. And they don't give up, emerging from the other end as proof their hope was warranted."

John Lane, Operations and Compliance Manager at Mini Excavations

"Optimism defines Faith in your ability and the support of your work team and family. Optimism is the precondition of human success.

Paul Mogote, Mogote Investment Partners

"The case for optimism is quite easy and can be found in the Bible. Spiritual optimism and a strong faith can lift one's life beyond imagination. Now if you're talking about the human condition- there will be technological progress, political jockeying, ideological battles, good vs. evil, and so on. Human nature has been pretty constant throughout time as we know it. Good luck."

Colonel Matthew T. Fritz

"I believe that optimism is born of hope: without either, there is no opportunity. Great leaders paint stories of hope, which sparks optimism in their teams to accomplish their mission and reach higher goals."

Konyka Dunson

"Knowing that my soul is tied to the unfathomable loving force of God, which causes the sun to rise gives me hope. No matter what happens, the sun rises each new day, and my soul rises with it. That knowledge gives me optimism that never ends."

Greg Sheridan, Writer

"Creation is good because God is good and he decided that creation would be good, so Genesis is not only rational but optimistic. The account in Genesis that God created humanity in his own image is the most powerful statement in favour of universal human rights that the ancient world ever saw."

Karen Stanford, Teacher

"Being an optimist I am lucky enough to see hope everywhere. Inspiring people following their dreams, people being kind to each other & as a teacher, the children give me reason to be optimistic every day"

Charlie Hogg, Brahma Kumaris

"The first relationship in life is with me. If this relationship is healthy, the mind creates an infectious perfume of positivity and a natural optimism that permeates the atmosphere and uplifts spirits."

Pope Francis

"Optimism is a human attitude that depends on so many things; but hope is something else: "it is a present, a gift of the Holy Spirit and for this reason Paul was to say that it never disappoints". It also has a name; and "this name is Jesus". It is impossible to say one hopes in life unless one hopes in Jesus. It would not be a question of hope rather, it would be good humour or optimism, as in the case of those sunny, positive people who always see a glass as half full and not half empty."

Loni and Rolf Uihlein

"Optimism is the base of our understanding of life. It depends on our belief in Christianity, independent of what mankind makes of it: katholisch, protestant or others. We are sure, that Jesus Christ has helped us through our long life… Sure, we have had many problems.. but we stand always together to overcome those."

Dr Paul Cooper, Associate Professor in Health Informatics

"Optimism must be based in your sense of what can best how people and organisations grow. Unbridled, unprincipled optimism is of no use to anyone if, like lemmings, it takes us over a cliff or doesn't lead to growth. A wonderful friend and mentor of mine Thomas Stianos told me years ago that the function of a leader is to provide hope for the future. These days I modify that quote a bit - to me the function of leadership is to ensure an abundance of opportunity for people. It's not enough to give hope, or have hope (unbridled optimism) - you must create the abundance that creates the opportunities for growth. This is hard work especially when things become tough (as they always will at some point). Fortunately, "abundance thinking" encourages people to share, and to give of their own energies and this is turn creates optimism. So breaking all this down, I think you need to first create opportunities for growth, people need to see that, believe in it, and then you can build the abundance. Optimism then flows from that."

Voices for Awakening of Consciousness

Adam Jacoby, Founder of MiVote

"The Case for Optimism? A global awakening of consciousness around the need for solutions orientation and a generation with a greater technological capability than any time in history."

Max Dumais, Thinker

"My optimism for the future grows with the arrival of each grandchild-this lot have definitely been here before! I have faith in the exponential growth of human consciousness as a counterpoint to entropy within the universe. While AI subsumes day to day operations on the planet I believe that the expansion of the capacity of the human brain has only just begun - perhaps even with artificial stimulation. My belief in an optimistic future is predicated on a faith in the upward and onward evolution of human consciousness."

Voices for Optimism of the Will

The Honourable Kim Beazley AC, Governor of Western Australia

"Anton Gramsci once said the correct position for a social democrat like myself was pessimism of the intellect but optimism of the will. Optimism without realism handicaps a society. Realism without optimism defeats it. In the confused world we inhabit it is the optimists who seize every opportunity for a constructive outcome. As a friend said of Winston Churchill's view in 1941 when all seemed bleak- his stance was *" something will turn up. Fight on and give it a chance*"."

Azra Raza, Oncologist and Author of The First Cell

"Antonio Gramsci famously imparted: "Pessimism of the intellect, optimism of the will." In other words, see the world as it really is, warts and all, but still forge ahead with courage, tenacity, persistence, acceptance. The will can overcome many challenges if hope remains alive."

Professor Roy Green, University of Technology Sydney

"I share with Antonio Gramsci an optimism of the will combined with pessimism of the intellect. There is no point in optimism unless it has some basis in reality, but likewise there is no point in the intellect unless it is directed towards a wider human purpose."

Simon Basketter, Journalist

"The Italian Marxist Antonio Gramsci argued that revolutionaries must stare reality in the face and find ways to push the class struggle forward. He borrowed the phrase, "pessimism of the intellect, optimism of the will" to deal with the problem. As a phrase it is a powerful warning against wishful thinking. And at the same time a cry against resignation. It proposes a determined, open-eyed engagement."

Gary Olson

"It's not entirely satisfying to say we need to do more but "optimism of the will" will help banish distractive pursuits. It's also what gives meaning to our lives."

Voices for Optimism and the Young

Paul Polman, former CEO of Unilever

"The future lies in the hands of the younger generation and that gives me huge cause for optimism. Wherever I go in the world, the young people I meet are engaged with the issues and challenges we face and focussed on finding solutions. Above all, they are driven by a deep sense of purpose. They may only represent 50% of today, but fortunately young people are 100% of tomorrow, and that is reason to celebrate".

Khayshie Tilak Ramesh, Victoria's Multicultural Youth Commissioner

"I am optimistic about the unknown. When we face uncertainty or the unknown, we have a choice to be afraid of what it entails or excited for the possibilities that it brings. I like to choose the latter - to be an optimist!"

Professor Raja Guha Thakurta, Astronomer at the UCO/Lick Observatory

"My optimism arises from the tremendous qualities I see in the young people I interact with. They are intelligent, passionate, motivated, hardworking, dedicated, ... they are capable of rising to meet any and every challenge. Our generation of adults has a responsibility of engaging youth in our work, sharing our passion and vision with them, and, equally importantly, learning about <u>their</u> passion and vision. It is clear to me that the future is in very good hands. We adults simply need to work with youth today to ensure that tomorrow's handover is a smooth one."

The Honourable Gabrielle Williams MP

"What makes me optimistic is our younger generation - a generation passionate about driving change, a generation committed to leaving the place better than they found it."

David Spence

"I'm optimistic that the next generation will be much smarter than the baby boomers. From management of natural resources to new productive ideas they are already proving themselves."

Stuart Allinson, Board Member ,Climate Change Authority

"I am continually impressed by this generation's ability to filter a vast amount of data, remove the noise and focus on the things that matter. Our generation had far fewer degrees of freedom to triangulate. The inter-generational constant is "glass half full vs glass half empty. Optimistic people are no more or less lucky than the rest of the population - they are more open to the possibilities that occur every day."

David Grieve, 5-dimensionz

"Leadership is essential in all levels of society, and some of the young people today have shown enormous goodwill and energy to provide service to those less fortunate than themselves."

Vivien Gardiner

The case for optimism lies in the young people of today, who are internet natives. They are not so bound, as their parents have been, by class, education, nationality, tradition. Their worldview and opportunities are expanded and their future, while challenging, is not so constrained by limited physical and social environments. Their communities cross many boundaries. They are cognisant of their own agency and of their "horizontal brotherhood". They have a heightened awareness of power structures and know how to avoid them if they choose to. Future adults will be more solutions-focused. They know the status quo isn't always to their benefit and that they have the power to resist it."

Sherilyn Hansen

“I am optimistic for the future because of the strength of character and commitment in young people. They are passionate, driven to create change but not at all costs - they will find the balance between economic good and social good and have a range of technology tools they have grown up with to help them get achieve their vision.”

Michelle Obama

“I’m optimistic about the future. There are some bright young people out there doing some amazing things. This is why I’m not going to run for president. Because I think it’s a better investment to invest in creating thousands of mes.”

Patrick Moore, President, Australian Institute of International Affairs

“The Case for optimism? Our Youth; many of which are fantastic.”

Keri Pratt

"Effective leadership is knowing when to listen and when to act and constantly fine-tuning the two. I
am optimistic that this balance is achievable and that there are many younger people who display this understanding."

Lesley Podesta, CEO of the Alannah & Madeline Foundation

“My optimism comes from the fact that we have the smartest, most educated generations coming up behind us and there is great contest of ideas and exciting growth and innovation from the growing middle classes in Asia and Africa. Borders mean something different to our children and the idea of the “ global citizen” is not theoretical anymore. I love that this change has largely been implemented without war or bloodshed but through ideas and communication.”

Maree Timms, Robotics Teacher

"Working with young people makes me optimistic. I never underestimate their drive, passion and tenacity when it comes to solving problems. The future is in good hands."

Mark J Bailey, Scientist

"Despite not having children, the youth of today make me optimistic. My case for optimism about a lot of things that people often seem pessimistic about is that by all metrics these things seem to be getting better: Crime, social justice etc. And what we can't fix will be fixed by the leaders of tomorrow, my nieces and nephews, my friends' children ..."

Ryan Bowler, Drama Teacher

"I am optimistic about the future that our younger citizens will shape because I see their optimism and hope on a daily basis."

Matthew Guy, Former Leader of the Liberal Party in the Victorian Parliament

"I'm very optimistic because I see Australian kids are vastly smarter, vastly more confident and vastly more ingenious than any generation we've ever seen. We should be confident about these young people and their ability to lead Australia better and differently in the decades ahead. I don't think my children's generation will be a pale imitation of mine or my parents' generation. I reckon they'll be something completely different. That's exciting!"

Bronwyn Leigh Jones, President, Coral Sustainable Services

"I am optimistic that our youth will nurture our planet back to good health. I am optimistic that our earth is surely in good hands with these bright, courageous souls guiding its evolution now and for the future."

Roqia Hashimi, Student, Shepparton High School

"Be optimistic and positive! First, know yourself: Without knowing your strengths and weaknesses it's pointless. Be patient: Life has its ups and downs you can't get to the top straight away. Falling down and picking yourself up helps you learn what helps you to rise with confidence."

Hanifa Haidary, Student, Shepparton High School

"What makes me optimistic is looking at the bright side of a dark day because I believe that's the only way we as individuals and the world will progress and better ourselves."

Patrick Bolton, Student, Goulburn Valley Grammar School

"What makes me optimistic? The knowledge that only I can decide whether I will be outworked or outsmarted. I have that choice."

Voices for Children and Optimism

Professor Lea Waters, Gerry Higgins Chair in Positive Psychology at the University of Melbourne

"Optimism is the most important psychological ingredient we can cultivate in our children. It is the secret weapon of strength-based parenting."

Catherine Misson

"If you look through the eyes of children you see limitless possibilities that tantalise the curious spirit with which they came into the world. How do we preserve that innate capacity? Optimism: enthusing our youth with an empowered view to the horizon no matter the challenges right in front of them. This is the source of our greatest potential as a society - optimistic citizens who believe they can and will craft a future worth inheriting."

Ashleigh Henrichs, Big Brothers and Big Sisters of Racine and Kenosha Counties

"Children will surprise you with their energy, optimism and hope. Who wouldn't want to be surrounded by hope these days?"

Camilla Schippa, Director, Institute for Economics and Peace

"When looking into a child's eye, how could we not be optimistic? We owe it to them, and to ourselves. Optimism is the essence of life, with it we move forward, without it, we stay still.

Paul King, President and CEO of Stanford Children's Health

"Pediatric medicine at its core is about optimism -- it's about the future."

Jennifer Vigne

"I do believe understanding levels of optimism, or lack thereof can be a solid indicator of how students can improve their academic performance, and how we as adults can optimize our own performance….Equipping our children with neurological lifelong tools like optimism, which can be practiced and improved over time, may not only make them happier, but studies show it will help them perform better in school. It will help them better overcome obstacles by viewing challenges as learning opportunities, and it will develop resilience when they've persevered through a difficult circumstance. To be clear, I'm not suggesting a Pollyanna view of the world but rather a healthy dose of balanced optimism that can help children and adults choose a more positive outlook."

Optimism, Creativity and Culture

Dave Holis, Disney Studios

"People are hungry for stories about optimism and hope"

Glenn Cole, 72andSunny

"Optimism is the ultimate creative act. It's imagining the best possible outcome or world without any constraints. When you create the conditions for it, you inspire others to move toward that future."

Kahlil Gibran, Author, The Prophet

"The optimist sees the rose and not its thorns; the pessimist stares at the thorns, oblivious to the rose."

Ava DuVernay

"Art calls to the optimism within us and beckons us to breathe"

Paul McCartney

"I am the eternal optimist. No matter how rough it gets, there's always light somewhere. The rest of the sky may be cloudy, but that little bit of blue draws me on."

Björk, Singer

"If optimism ever was like an emergency, it's now. Instead of moaning and becoming really angry, we need to actually come up with suggestions of what the world we want to live in, in the future, could be."

Femi Kuti, Nigerian Singer-Songwriter

"To be optimistic is to fully understand the true meaning of our existence. Optimism is the mechanism of creation. Without optimism, nothing would exist."

Miho Hatori

"We need the freedom to express. We cannot be passive from society's energy. We can be independent. That's my way of thinking of new optimism."

August Greene with Brandy

Optimism (The Song)

Chorus:
You can win
As long as you keep your head to the sky
Be optimistic

Verse 1
When in the midst of sorrow
You can't see up when looking down
A brighter day tomorrow will bring
Hey yeah, yeah
You hear the voice of reason
Telling you this cannot weigh me down
No matter how hard reality seems
Just hold on to your dreams, yeah

Verse 2
Don't give up and don't give in
Although it seems you never win
You will always pass the test
As long as you keep your head to the sky
You can win
As long as you keep your head to the sky
You can win
As long as you keep your head to the sky
Be optimistic

Charlotta Efverman, Swedish-Australian Crime Novelist

"In my line of work, I research the most horrific acts of violence that people inflict on other people - and you might think that seeing the worst in people darkens my perception of the world; but it doesn't. I know there are dark and light sides in all of us - and a whole lot of grey shades in between.... I choose to see the light side in most people and situations; because I know there are dark storms in every life - and it's how we choose to deal with these situations that determine what sort of people we are. We build our own reality in our thoughts - and we then operate from this reality when we contribute to the world we live in: in our actions. This story of an old Aboriginal man who sits by the fire with his young grandson describes my view of how we choose to see the world: The grandfather turns his gaze from the fire, looks into his grandson's eyes and solemnly says: "There are two dingoes constantly fighting inside every man and woman. One dingo is called 'Good' and the other one is called 'Evil'." The young boy curiously asks: "Which dingo wins?" The old man's eyes reflect sadness as he replies: "The one you feed."

Mariah Carey, Singer

"The thing that some people don't realise, we are all just people. Everybody has their own stuff that they deal with, grew up dealing with, just any type of adversity that you have to overcome. We all go through things and that's part of life. The main thing is to stay hopeful and optimistic."

Terry Crews, actor, former NFL player

I stay positive by actually choosing things to be thankful for. An attitude of gratitude literally gives you energy. But I also found that I used to be the opposite. And my wife will tell you, 'cause we've been married 28 years, she knows the other side. I was not a nice person to live with. And when I saw, personally, the differences in my life from once I was a pessimist to the switch to being an optimist, it's like night and day. Instead of looking for what's wrong with everything, I started to look for what was right with everything. And you start to realise that you only get where your habits take you. So, the way you think gets you what you want in life. If you think everybody is against you, if you think you're not going to get something, usually you don't. And it kinda becomes a self-fulfilling prophecy. But when I started shifting and saying, "OK, I'ma go into this place like they want to see me" and say "Hey! Wait! Things are going to be better." All of a sudden, things got better.

Charlie Jane Anders, Science Fiction Author

"Writing a dystopian story is really an optimistic act. It is based on the idea that we can confront this dark possibility and actually face up to and possibly do something about it."

Eilleen Shields, ICT Consultant

I have thought for over a week on the challenge of contributing a quote for "hope and optimism". My quest ended in a song by John Lennon ... which sums it up I believe:

Imagine no possessions
I wonder if you can
No need for greed or hunger
A brotherhood of man
Imagine all the people
Sharing all the world
You, you may say I'm a dreamer
But I'm not the only one
I hope someday you will join us
And the world will live as one

Ayse Birsel, Speaker

"Optimism is one of the core strengths of designers. We inherently believe that no matter how hard the problem, we will come up with a better solution and this optimism drives our energy and our passion."

Salman Farooqi, Artist, Pakistan

"Over the last 20 to 25 years, I have been an optimist and a believer in life. My works are, consequently, optimistic, bright and cheerful. I do not wish to convey sadness through art and I strive to depict beauty, energy and vitality that is not readily visible in everyday scene. My paintings are designed to be celebrations of happiness, positivity and cheerfulness."

Joan Ormrod, Senior Lecturer, Manchester Metropolitan University

"A messiah figure like Superman is an icon that inspires renewal, optimism and hope. In an age of fake news, violence and cynicism, this is surely a significant reason for his persistence as a symbol of heroism."

Sigrid Thornton, Australian actress

"My own life is a bit paradoxical. I am sentimental and I can lean towards nostalgia. But really I'm quite a genuine optimist. And when you're an optimist you need to keep putting one foot in front of the other."

Dana Al Fardan, Qatar's (only) female contemporary composer

"Having started to export my music internationally and been overwhelmed by the positive response received, I have been struck by a sincere sense of optimism. This feeling stems from a true belief in the unique power of music to act as a universal, unifying force. As a global community we need no common language, nationality, political persuasion or race, to be brought together in our enjoyment of music. It is that timeless quality that encourages my optimism for music as an art form and as a business; we can always turn to music as a therapy, to unite us as human beings, and to provide the soundtrack to the landmark events of our lives."

Optimistic Plays and Music

Joshua Kosman, Classical Music Critic

"Candide' celebrates the magic of boundless optimism."

Sheryl Flatow

Candide concerns the travels and travails of a callow youth who remains eternally optimistic under the worst circumstances, thanks to the teachings of a not-so-sage philosopher, Dr. Pangloss.

Vikki Broughton Hodges, Writer on the optimism of "Annie"

"The movie (Annie) was based on a popular musical that won seven Tony Awards when it premiered in 1977, including Best Musical, and ran for nearly six years on Broadway because of its positive message about optimism in the face of adversity — the setting is New York City during the Great Depression and the lead character is an orphan looking for a family... Annie's sense of optimism is an uplifting part of the musical that sends people home with a smile on their face."

Timothy Tuller, Saint John's Cathedral

"Edward Elgar's mammoth Symphony No. 1 ... This late-Romantic masterpiece... brimming with an undisputedly English sense of nobility and optimism in the face of adversity. An orchestral music lover's dream, it is a piece that puts every section of the orchestra through its paces."

Katie Knight on Amélie The Musical

"at its heart is a story of relentless optimism– and this is portrayed in such a touching, genuine manner, it is sure to stay with its audiences long after."

Mark Hamill, Actor: Luke Skywalker in the Star Wars

"I was the most optimistic, hopeful character."

Toni Morrison, Author and Nobel laureate

"Of course I am a storyteller and therefore an optimist , a firm believer in the ethical bend of the human heart , a believer in the mind's appetite for truth and its disgust with fraud. I'm a believer in the power of knowledge and the ferocity of beauty, so from my point of view your life is already artful — waiting, just waiting, for you to make it art."

Compliments and Phrases

I read widely on optimism and have collected some delightful phrases on optimism and optimistic people. If you can fit in an optimism word or phrase into any piece of writing, you will lift the reader. As Dr. KH Kim wrote, "Research has shown that you can develop your optimistic attitude by practicing positive speech and actions in everyday activities. Then, refine your outlook by taking a positive path forward in every circumstance"

Here are a few phrases I have collected – please quote them or use them in your writing. Indeed, think of doing that with any of the quotes in this book which inspire you.

Phrases

Susan Lewis

"I feel as if I have indeed been given a gift; a sense of optimism, that I and others have the power, and responsibility, to make a difference."

Jennifer Hermes Nastu, Content Director

"I feel a great sense of optimism. We can do this. We are doing this."

Governor Gina Raimondo, Rhode Island

“ I’m filled with optimism because I’ve seen what we can accomplish together.”

Karissa Niehoff

"I promise to be respectful about the past, realistic about the present & optimistic about the future."

Edith Perez, former president of the Los Angeles Police Commission

“I guess I have a perennially optimistic view of accomplishing what I set out to do."

Stuart Steen McFaull @Steenmonkey

"It's a heartening feeling, renewed optimism coursing through my veins"

John Madison

“The contagious fire of optimism amidst a world of pessimism"

People Against Dirty

“a company… filled with fearless thinkers, mad scientists and adventurous designers who believe in defying the status quo with innovation and optimism.”

Zach Buckley

“The sweet nectar of unbridled optimism"

Daniel Gallan

“There was unbridled optimism as they set sail towards an unknown horizon"

Kate Snyder

"I’m a pretty serious optimist. I sometimes joke that my rose-colored glasses are bulletproof"

“To my fellow optimists — here’s to us! We believe that the world is beautiful and we’re obstinate enough to make it so"

Governor Charlie Baker

"Let’s make our brand of politics positive and optimistic, instead of cruel and dark"

Governor Jay Inslee

“It’s about talking about the level of our ambition, and the level of our commitment to our kids, and the level of our sense of optimism. We have to have a vision of the future rather than just a concern about the future. We’ve got to have a positive statement of a way forward rather than just a warning sign.”

Nicola Sturgeon, Scotland's First Minister

"I'm a fully paid up believer in the power of optimism in politics."

Richard Spires and Sean Morgan on Cybersecurity

"the crucial need for a healthy infusion of optimism and bold, unconventional thinking to tackle the central challenge of our era."

Vasudha Gulati

"awash with optimistic energy"

Prayer in The Fairmont News

"And we hope and pray that your hope and optimism floods the world with peace, love, compassion and grace, and effects real, positive change for generations to come."

Jenny Henders writing about a speech by Cathy Heron

"An ode to optimism"

Job Advertisement

Applicant should engage "people positively, with a demeanor of optimism and abundance."

Origins Forgotten

"An Air of Optimism"

"An overriding feeling of joy, hope, and optimism"

"a renewed sense of optimism among the staff so they'll be thinking about what they can do instead of what they can't because of personnel or infrastructure shortages."

"We take nothing for granted, but we feel very optimistic about the opportunity"

"A renewed sense of optimism"

"A sense of optimism for what is possible in this region"

"A sense of optimism through empowerment"

"I am quite optimistic this meeting will yield positive results."

"Houses the future in sustainable optimism"

"Optimism and hope are laced through, peeking like sunlight through blinds."

Compliments

Sir David Attenborough

"while there are people like you putting your heads together, people like you getting together and spending time together, it does seem to me, as an onlooker, that the world has a cause for optimism and cause for gratitude."

Priscilla Runion on Assuming We Survive

"Each and every aspect of their existence is infused with that collective energy and unbridled optimism."

Brandon Cigana speaking of John Hoague-Rivette

"He has been a beacon of optimism since I've ever known him"

Ray Routhier on Susan Conley

"Susan has an incredible energy. She has a great work ethic and sense of optimism."

Jus Armour speaking of Tony Kalathara

"his inherent, contagious optimism"

Joel Edward Goza on Martin Luther King

"King was intimate with mountaintop moments when hope and optimism harmonized"

Cathal Dennehy

"Even the most sceptical judge couldn't help but raise an optimistic eyebrow at the breadth of brilliance."

'Julia' on author Mason Deaver

"When I think of Nathan, I think of warmth. Of reds, and oranges. But most of all, I think of yellow. That just seems like such a Nathan-y color. Happiness, joy, his optimism, that smile."

John Bryant

"I am filled with gratitude for your work, inspired by your leadership, and optimistic about our course for the future."

Malcolm Turnbull, former Australian Prime Minister

"Thank you for your hard work and your optimism"

Optimists' Obituaries

"Mandela's relentless optimism and struggle for human rights and freedom are a source of inspiration for all"
On Nelson Mandela

“Integrity, optimism and an unwavering patriotic streak were his hallmark.”
C.V. Aravind on Arun Jaitley

“I think the thing that's understated the most is his optimism. That's what made John special, made John a giant among all of us.”
Joe Biden on John McCain

“He had been to hell and back and yet somehow never lost his energy or his optimism or his zest for life. So cancer did not scare him"
Barack Obama on Senator John McCain

"The horizons he saw were bright and hopeful. He was a genuinely optimistic man, and that optimism guided his children and made each of us believe that anything was possible." George W. Bush on George H.W. Bush

"Throughout his life, in the midst of the most difficult trials, he always looked to the future with a spirit of optimism, faith, and love."
Renzo Allegri on Saint Padre Pio

"His eternal optimism, kindness and competitiveness inspired us always to reach higher."
Oklahoma A&M Board of Regents and Chairman Tucker Link on T. Boone Pickins

"Optimistic, brilliant, diplomatic and kind, Steve led by bringing out the very best qualities of those around him."
Ron Richard on Steven Minter

"He brought joy and a magnetic optimism to all who knew him and was a loyal friend to many."
On Mark Cox

"She was still the life of the party, full of joy, optimism and sweetness."
Stacey Mollus on Carol Dupree

"The ultimate optimist, her smile brightened rooms and melted hearts as she touched, then impacted every life that crossed her path."
On Martha Scharbauer Adams

“His infectious energy and optimistic spirit have helped LiveLaw outgrow its phases of uncertainty and doubt.”
M A Rashid on Professor Shamnad Basheer

“He had a generous spirit with infectious optimism. His influence will remain in the lives of those who knew him.”
On James Winston Hayes

“She was a vibrant fountain of happiness and optimism.”
On Marilyn Smith Gattis

“Jerry was a real believer in God and in the goodness and potential of his fellow man, a super optimist every day of his life, always happy, always positive, always encouraging and loving others.“
On Jerry Tapp

Optimistic Humour

The optimist says the glass is half full.
The pessimist says the glass is half empty.
The engineer says the glass is over-designed for the quantity of water.

The optimist says the glass is half full.
The pessimist says the glass is half empty.
The communist says the glass is too full, and needs to be redistributed among the other glasses.

The optimist says the glass is half full.
The pessimist says the glass is half empty.
The worrier frets that the remaining half will evaporate by morning.

The optimist says the glass is half full.
The pessimist says the glass is half empty.
The auditor first checks whether the empty half is material and then designs the audit procedures to obtain sufficient evidence to conclude that the glass is indeed empty.

The optimist says the glass is half full.
The pessimist says the glass is half empty.
The entrepreneur sees the glass as undervalued by half its potential.

The optimist says the glass is half full.
The pessimist says the glass is half empty.
The inquisitive troublemaker wants to know what's in the glass anyhow...

The optimist says the glass is half full.
The pessimist says the glass is half empty.
The physicist says that the glass is not empty at all - it is half-filled with water and half-filled with air - hence, fully filled on the whole!

The optimist says the glass is half full.
The pessimist says the glass is half empty.
The project manager says the glass is twice as big as it needs to be.

The optimist says the glass is half full.
The pessimist says the glass is half empty.
The pedant says the glass contains half the required amount of liquid for it to overflow.

The optimist says the glass is half full.
The pessimist says the glass is half empty.
The seminar presenter does not care if the glass is half full or half empty, he just knows that starting the discussion will give him ten minutes to figure out why his PowerPoint presentation is not working.

Miz Feiler, Blogger

My mother is an optimistic. She taught me to be one too. But now that I am a mother, also juggling a business and a multitude of daily tasks, I understand that it is not always enough for one's glass to be half full. Sometimes you need to fill that wine glass right to the top.

Sean Doran, Educator, Author, Possibilitarian

"An optimist or pessimist the difference is rather droll... the optimist sees the doughnut, the pessimist the hole. Nothing is more linked to success than optimism. It's a skill that can, and should be taught in schools."

Source Unknown

"An optimist is someone who brings a book to read for an eye dilation test"

Conclusion

I trust and hope you have enjoyed this book and the contributions of hundreds of people relating to optimism. My request of that you use your learning on a daily basis to increase the optimism of those around you.

Please feel free to join our movement for optimism. There are entire sections of the global economy devoted to exploiting fear, anxiety and pessimism to sell goods and services and we need to help people rise above that. Pessimism leads to paralysis and we see this in climate fear, political cynicism and postmodern distrust of people and institutions.

Make sure optimism is a theme or sub-theme of every conference, retreat and meeting you have a role in organising.

Please help us get the message out there through social media, video conferencing and the like.

I always welcome engagement whether it's new perspectives or questions.

My website is www.victorperton.com and there's a wealth of contemporary content including meditations and links to assist and help you get in contact with me.

Remember, the leader looks like the person in your mirror.

Remember to ask people what makes them optimistic.

Remember to use the phrase, "I am optimistic about...."

Thanks

The first thank you is to my colleagues on the Advisory Board of the Global Integrity Conference who agreed to optimism as a theme and as the final session in 2017. As the Chair Paul Mazerolle said, "Optimism for the future is the recognition that our progress as a global community requires human ingenuity, creativity, innovation, knowledge, partnerships, tolerance and values. Progress is not inevitable. It requires commitment, actions over words, good deeds over promises, as well as proactive responses and co-active efforts. Despite the challenges and setbacks across the 20 century, the achievements over the past hundred years are remarkable. I am optimistic for the future because of my fundamental belief in the skills, values, and commitment of people to make a difference for the world, supported by the wider community in enacting or supplying resources and conditions to enable human flourishing to endure. Long may it continue!"

Thanks to my Mother Lilia who has been a source of inspiration and optimism all my life. A refugee who lived under the dictatorships of Stalin and Hitler, she has helped lift thousands of people through her tireless advocacy of yoga as a way of life.

To my sister Regina who provided many good ideas during the drafting of this book and my many presentations.

Thanks to Ted and Sophia who are infectiously optimistic and share their three blessings with me on a daily basis.

Support for This Project

Danielle Guttman-Klein

“Victor, You are my North Star on optimism. You have an innate capability of understanding issues and circumstance, and spinning the solution in a positive, collective and realistic fashion. It is no surprise to me that you are taking a strong lead in an optimistic movement and I am certain, with your energy and commitment that optimism will prevail.”

Shane Oliver

“Great project! Unfortunately Australia seems lost in the mire of pessimism all too much lately.”

Peter Kronborg, Chair, Wise Counsel Associates

"Consider Optimism as the top end of a simple straight bar magnet. It is an invisible energy that attracts good and feels good. And Pessimism is at the other end. It repels and feels bad. We can’t always be at the optimistic end but if we generally flow and feel into that energy then Like will attract Like. Simple ! Victor's book helps polish the top of our life magnet ! Love it."

Alma Besserdin

"Thank you for including me in your project. Everything starts with great leadership. I am so passionate about it!"

Donna Petrovich

"I am optimistic and appreciate your work Victor"

Natalie Scanlon

"Thank you so much for asking for my contribution. It really means a lot to me."

Joan Fitzpatrick

"Thanks for inviting me to contribute – how kind you are. Also, big congratulations for this initiative, in a world full of awful news and a constant stream of stories about human misery and fear, it's important for us to remind ourselves about optimism and indeed hope."

Gretha Oost

"Brilliant, let's spread the word about optimism"

Gus Buckner, Author of the P'fessor Guus books including "An Essential Book of Good"

"May you continue to be blessed with much love, peace, joy, well-being & prosperity.... Because you are truly amazing !! Thank you !!!! "

Peter Wegner

"A noble cause you are promoting! I stay as optimistic as they come, having gone through the wars, - but changing the world to have more integrity will not happen in my lifetime."

Paula Dunn

"Funny it gets me thinking about Leadership in a more profound way. Awesome!

Chris Drake

"thank you for the inspiration to think a little bit about optimism."

Karina Wegner, Psychologist

"It is funny that commonsense is not so common ! Your discussion on optimism is awesome, so why don't people get it? I wrote my Master's Thesis about optimism with Martin Seligman as one of my supervisors and nothing has changed in 25 years. If you have not read "Brainwise Leadership" please do as it is based on common-sense written by Connie Henson and Pieter Rossouw."

Mignon and John Wegner

"It is certainly a good time for a little optimism."

Tony Harding

"This wide-ranging book is thought provoking, and, as you would expect, certainly optimistic in tone! Views on optimism from a diverse range of people are quoted. Links to leadership, technology and learned optimism are also discussed as well as cultural differences e.g. between USA and Australia. Highly recommended."

Diana Hodgson

"I was honoured to be invited by Victor Perton to contribute to The Case for Optimism. Optimism is a very powerful mindset and driver for the positive change that is possible!"

Billie Giles-Corti

"Congratulations Victor – this is a wonderful achievement."

Armando Gonzalo Alvarez Reina, Ambassador of Mexico to Australia

"Optimism is precisely what we need more in these times."

Monica Bennett

"Well done Victor, a big achievement!"

Emily Harrison

I think the case for optimism, in our world today, is needed now more than ever."

Matthew Reddy

"We need more senior voices with experience sharing wisdom."

Mariano Fabrizio

"Good to learn you have published this book. A very interesting topic indeed. As I was going over the sample pages, I thought about myself, my career, my goals in life, and came up to the conclusion that I have been very optimistic myself. I think optimism is a state of mind that works as the underlying asset of every single project, the pillars upon which you can build an empire."

Major General Vinod Saighal

Victor, you have undertaken a very endearing burden upon yourself because optimism is the only antidote to the depression, dejection and hopelessness that has enmeshed large portions of the globe due to poverty and exacerbated by wars that keep recurring somewhere or the other. On the face of it you might be fighting a losing battle because hopelessness is the order of the day. Most of the rejects of society do not see light at the end of the tunnel. It is not easy to reassure them. Between optimism and pessimism at either extreme lies realism. 15000 scientists have recently signed a plea for the world leaders cautioning - warning them really - that humanity is fast reaching the point of irreversibility unless we immediately change course. Easier said than done when every world leader of the big powers and the smaller ones for that matter is engulfed in looking at his own miserable survival at the helm. One can go on in this vein. I will not do so because the human race as a collectivity has it in its power to save itself from obliteration. Your book underpins that aspiration."

Elizabeth Vega

"Thank you for including my contribution. I'm very pleased that it is helpful and relevant. There is just too much energy & focus invested in agonising over things outside of our control. We all know that the world is inherently uncertain, and unstable & we need to prioritise getting on with the best of the opportunities right in front of us. The fact that you value my opinion is in itself a cause for me to feel optimistic."

Miriam Feiler

"I love Helen Clark's comment, *"Good things happen when good people get together in common cause."* I couldn't agree more. For us at bizzi, great things happen when businesses collaborate!"

Jagdeep Bhatia, Founder, Australian Sandalwood Soap Factory

"It was quiet fascinating to read what the deep power of Optimism meant to so many influential individuals. Interesting reading and even appreciated by my teenage daughter who now stole it from me. LOL"

Sean Doran

“I read your book last night Victor and was engrossed . Such an inspiration - you should be very proud of it - I think I we should be teaching optimism in schools.”

Professor Marcia Devlin

"The work of Victor Perton on optimism in leadership is inspiring."

Other Books to Read

For sound advice in increasing your level of optimism, it's worth reading "Learned Optimism: How to Change Your Mind and Your Life" by Martin Seligman or his later book "Flourish."

Another good guide is Harvard Medical School's "Positive Psychology: Harnessing the power of happiness, mindfulness, and inner strength."

Made in the USA
San Bernardino, CA
05 November 2019

59534055R00175